SO-ATU-265

CURING SUNDAY SPECTATORITIS

From Passivity to Participation in Church

By

Larry Peabody

7509 Magnolia Ct. SE

Lacey, WA 98503

(360) 459-2031

Urban Loft Publishers | Skyforest, CA

Patrick,
Grateful for
your vision
of God's purposes
for his people!
Blessings!
Larry

Curing Sunday Spectatoritis
From Passivity to Participation in Church

Copyright © 2016 Larry Peabody.
All rights reserved. No part of this book may be reproduced in
any manner without prior written permission from the
publisher.

Bakke Graduate University Press
An Imprint of Urban Loft Publishers

Write: Permissions, Urban Loft Publishers, P.O. Box 6,
Skyforest, CA, 92385.
Urban Loft Publishers
P.O. Box 6
Skyforest, CA. 92385
www.urbanloftpublishers.com

ISBN: 978-0-9973717-3-4
Manufactured in the U.S.A

Editors: Stephen Burris & Kendi Howells Douglas
Track Coordinator: Susan Spousta
Copy Editor: Adrienn Vasquez
Graphics: Elisabeth Clevenger

Unless otherwise indicated, all Scripture quotations are from
THE HOLY BIBLE, NEW INTERNATIONAL VERSION®, NIV®
Copyright © 1973, 1978, 1984, 2011 by Biblica, Inc.® Used by
permission. All rights reserved worldwide.

ENDORSEMENTS

Curing Sunday Spectatoritis takes seriously the often neglected key biblical theme of one-another behaviors and practices. Offered by a seasoned pastor with a wealth of practical experience, this survey of worship patterns in two dozen churches gives us an intriguing album of pictures of congregations that have discovered what real Christian community can mean practically. Peabody shows that deep sharing and true koinonia really can happen in relatively large congregational gatherings. It does not have to be limited to small groups, essential as they are. The book thus projects a healthy balance that can help churches today discover the depths of community and mutual discipling that so many churches lack.

Howard A. Snyder,

Visiting Director, Manchester Wesley Research Centre, England

If you have even a shred of Christ's love for the church you will find this book riveting. It is not simply a rant about what has gone wrong but a wonderful discovery of what is so right about the church born in the love and mission of God. Larry Peabody pleads for a shift from spectatoritis to living out the "one-anothers" of Scripture. After all, no New Testament Christian went to church to worship (of course they did when together) because they were already worshipping all week long (Romans 12:1-2). What they did when they came together was to engage in mutual edification, the very thing most lacking in church meetings today. This is the nub of the gathered church and Peabody elaborates on this not just with biblical fidelity and careful reasoning but helpful illustrations of churches actually functioning this way. Read and be prepared for a renewal. After all, As Peabody says, "And could it be that the relationships of costly, self-giving love provide the best clue as to why the first-century church grew at such an astounding pace?"

R. Paul Stevens,

Professor Emeritus, Marketplace Theology, Regent College

Chairman, Institute for Marketplace Transformation

In *Curing Sunday Spectatoritis* Larry Peabody tells us what we know – that monological churches do not produce healthy communities and vigorous Christian disciples. He also demonstrates that multivoiced alternatives are possible. Peabody uses the bible extensively and convincingly, showing that he has entered empathetically into the ethos of the early churches. He also draws upon the writings of scholars and practitioners; the literature in this area is surprisingly large! And he makes his case convincingly because he bases it on his own wide experience and illustrates it with stories of two dozen churches who are learning how to leave clericalism behind. This book makes a strong contribution, and I recommend it highly.

Alan Kreider,

Anabaptist Mennonite Biblical Seminary, author of The Patient Ferment of the Early Church, and of Worship and Mission after Christendom (with Eleanor Kreider)

"This is a convincing case for churches to make the profound shift to congregational participation. Case studies from round the world show how this can work in practice, and how churches come alive in the process. An inspirational window on the work of God's Spirit today."

Jeremy Thomson,

Author of Preaching as Dialogue, Head of Practical Theology (Vice Principal), Oasis College of Higher Education, London

Curing Sunday Spectatoritis

Curing Sunday Spectatoritis is a book for pastors and church members who are convinced they need to engage the whole church in the work and life of the church. This book is a comprehensive tool kit full of quotes and proofs, stories and Bible passages, concrete ideas and vision that can be used in sermons, leadership meetings, small groups, and coffee conversations to ignite change to cure the serious disease of passive consumerism in the church. As I read the 24 case studies of real churches who are seriously curing this disease, I kept thinking "Why didn't we think of that?" and "I've got to share this in the next leaders meeting."

Brad Smith,

President, Bakke Graduate University

Expect this book to challenge your thoughts about the very structures of life in traditional churches that foster the disease of *spectatoritis*. Larry Peabody invites us to view a broad landscape of church life: fresh insights into biblical passages, historical reflections that trace how we got to where we are, a wealth of quotations from influential voices, and powerful examples from two dozen churches. It may not take you a long time to read this well-written, thought provoking, practical, hope-filled book – but plan to spend a lot of time in prayerful reflection on how you might take new steps into a richly rewarding journey of doing church together – with one another!

Leland V. Eliason, ThD,

Executive Director and Provost Emeritus, Bethel Seminary of Bethel University;

Founding Dean, School of Ministry, Richmont Graduate University

TABLE OF CONTENTS

Foreword...10

Introduction 13

Chapter 1 18

   Spectatoritis vs. One-Anothering...18

      Warnings from Older Voices // 19

      Concern Continues in Younger Voices // 21

      Treating Sunday Spectatoritis // 22

      The New Command // 24

      New Recipients of the Loving // 25

      New Standard for the Loving // 26

      New Results of the Loving // 26

      Trinitarian One-Anothering // 27

      One-Anothering and the Great Commission // 29

      One-Anothering as the Reason for Gathering // 31

      Participatory Gathering Meets a Roadblock // 33

Chapter 2..35

   Meetings Shaped by Tradition 35

      Characteristics of McDonaldization // 36

      McDonaldization in the Church // 37

      What Forces Shape Our Gatherings? // 40

      The Worship Maxim // 41

      Why Should We Gather? // 43

      Other Voices on Why We Meet // 45

      The Architectural Effect // 48

      Church or Theater? // 48

      What Theaters Foster // 52

Curing Sunday Spectatoritis

The Liturgical Lockstep // 54

The Case for Conventional Liturgy // 57

The Case against Conventional Liturgy // 58

The Leadership Focus // 61

The Silencing of the Laity // 61

A Water Shortage // 65

Church Traditions: A Structure Too Small // 66

Chapter 3..68

Making Disciples in Church as We Know It.......................68

Alike Yet Different // 70

What Going to Church Now Means to Nearly Everyone // 75

The Elephant Won't Go Away // 76

Making the Best Use of Our Time Together // 80

Chapter 4..87

The Case for One-Anothering as We Gather 87

Growth Happens as Christ Reveals Himself through His Body // 89

Each Part a Working Part // 90

Creating a One-Anothering Environment // 94

One-Anothering Takes Knowing Each Other // 96

One-Anothering and the Kingdom of God // 98

A Kingdom-Related One-Anothering Strategy // 99

Chapter 5..101

One-Anothering Actions 101

Greeting One Another // 102

Praying For One Another // 104

Encouraging One Another // 105

Spurring One Another On // 106

Teaching/Instructing One Another // 108

Serving One Another // 111

Confessing Sins to One Another // 113

Chapter 6...**117**

One-Anothering in Churches.. 117

Axiom Church, Syracuse, NY // 119

Bethany Baptist Church, Puyallup, WA // 124

Christ Church Deal, Deal, Kent, UK // 127

Church for Men, an Online Blog // 128

Community Church of Hayward, CA // 130

Elim Evangelical Free Church, Puyallup, WA // 131

First Covenant Church of St. Paul, St. Paul, MN // 133

Grace Community Church, Gresham, OR // 135

Jacob's Well Church, Chicago, IL // 138

The Kingdom Citizens' Pavilion, Jos, Nigeria // 142

Lacey Presbyterian Church, Lacey, WA // 145

Mill City Church, Minneapolis, MN // 152

Neighborhood Alliance Church *(now Sojourn)*, Lacey, WA // 156

Network Church, St. Albans, UK // 158

New Day Church, Tacoma, WA // 162

Northwood Church, Maple Grove, MN // 165

Peniel Wesleyan Tabernacle, Greater Georgetown, Guyana // 171

Salvation Army Berry Street Worship Center, Nashville, TN // 172

Sampa Community Church, Sao Paulo, Brazil // 174

Sumas Advent Christian Church, Sumas, WA // 179

Temple Baptist Church, Rockford, IL // 182

The Church on the Way, Van Nuys, CA // 183

The Evergreen Community, Portland, OR // 185

Westview Bible Church, Pierrefonds, Quebec, Canada // 191

Wild Goose Christian Community, Indian Valley, Floyd County, VA // 195

Chapter 7...**200**

Preparing the Congregation... 200

Curing Sunday Spectatoritis

Welcoming the Holy Spirit and His Gifts // 202

Hearing God Speak // 204

Practicing the Priesthood of All Believers // 207

Discovering Calling // 212

Understanding the Biblical Role of Pastors // 215

Serving the Church in Both Its Modes // 218

Seeing All of Life through the Kingdom Lens // 220

Recognizing and Reporting on the Providence of God // 222

Reasonable Reminders // 224

The Magnitude of Making the Transition // 225

Appendix A: 227

FaithStory Presentation Guidelines, ... 227

Northwood Church, Maple Grove, MN 227

Appendix B: 230

Our Journey in Implementing Participatory Meetings 230

References 234

About the Author 242

FOREWORD

Curing Spectatoritis is part of an Urban Loft/BGU.edu imprint series focused on global urban leadership, yet it is also a book that applies to every church, big or small, rural or urban, global north or global south. This is not an urban ministry book, but it has particular application to the needs of urban churches.

Global demographic studies show that since the early 2000s the majority of the world now lives in cities. After centuries of humans mostly living in rural settings, cities are growing at a whirlwind pace in almost every part of the world. Yet, not only is the majority of the world now living in urban densities, the rest of the world is affected by urban mindsets. Global media, entertainment, popular culture, education, and government policies are increasingly instruments of urbanization – spreading urban culture far into rural areas. Today, any church leader located in almost any location needs to understand the influence of urbanization to effectively lead their congregation to influence the world around them. It is harder for any church to say that it is not urban since the influence of mass urbanization is so pervasive.

Additionally, churches in cities are located in places that have many more competing and confusing world views. This creates great pressure to create a church-based safe haven from this urban complexity. Such a safe haven would be full of programs for consumers of religions goods and services that would allow these consumers to live lives as separate as possible from the confusion around them. Christian consumers carry their lifestyle of being entertained and catered to outside the church into their expectations of what inside the church should look like. The greater the pressure surrounding the church, the more consumer-oriented the culture is, and the more resources the church has to create large staffs, buildings and buffer programs, the more they are susceptible to spectatoritis. Churches in cities often have the pressure and the financial resources to be a rich breeding ground for the crippling disease of spectatoritis.

Yet with the great challenge comes great opportunity. Urban churches have so many more opportunities to be instruments of salt and light in their community. There are more eyes on them. When they steward well, their influence in the more complex systems of power, money and human sexuality that surround them creates a vibrant contrast to what the rest of the world is doing. People watching become angry and hostile or intrigued and attracted. It is a great opportunity to display the gospel.

To do this well in the midst of an urban context that has more competing voices, more complexity, and more avenues for influence means that more of the church has to be involved in the neighborhood and city where the church is located. For this to work, more church members need to be actively doing the work of the church both in the church gathered on the weekend and also—especially—in the church scattered throughout the week.

Curing Sunday Spectatoritis

That is why *Curing Sunday Spectatoritis* is a book that is so relevant to churches located in cities. It is not an exclusively urban book but it certainly is a necessary urban book.

Brad Smith, President, Bakke Graduate University (BGU.edu)

INTRODUCTION

How can we open church worship services to congregational participation?

This was the basic question posed to pastors and church leaders as I researched this book. Thankfully, I learned that some are finding creative ways to increase involvement. As the examples in this book demonstrate, churches in a variety of contexts are making it possible for members of Christ's body to hear from each other in the main congregational meeting. From an under-resourced neighborhood in Syracuse, NY, to a multi-staffed church in Gresham, OR, to an Appalachian community in Indian Valley, VA, 25 churches show how.

Both that opening question and this entire book concern church *practice*. Countless numbers of churches hold Scripture to be our only rule for faith and practice. The same churches usually issue statements of faith, but how often have you read a church statement of practice? These chapters deal not with what we *believe* (vital) but with what we *do* (equally vital). Specifically, the book zeroes in on what we do when we gather. The contrast between the gathering practice of the early church and what takes place in most contemporary churches has long concerned me. To oversimplify, it seems that centuries ago the Church traded participation by the people for performance by the professionals. The Church—and the world we are here to illuminate—are both reaping the consequences of that exchange today.

These chapters were born out of a love for the Church. Much that is good takes place in our twenty-first century gatherings. So I see the Church as a glass half full. But that leaves the other half as an unfilled potential. All of us must cope with an inherited church culture that can and does affect the wellness of the Church. The word "curing" in the title points to both diagnosis and treatment. Many parts of contemporary church culture promote the health of Christ's body and need to be preserved. But those that work against its well-being—including any that weaken the body of Christ with spectatoritis—need to be recognized and remedied.

One pastor told me he knew of just one way to increase bonding in large congregations: "Divide the members into small cell groups, and encourage them to be more faithful to the small group than to the bigger crowd." He added, "I'm not against large churches, but connectedness can never happen in a large crowd." I suspect he speaks for many pastors.

For some, the idea of congregational participation in the main weekly meeting brings up some not-so-pleasant memories. A seminary official told me, "When I have been in a church where there is an 'open mic' time, the sharing is seldom about anything except sickness and personal problems." This book offers evidence it does not have to work that way.

It also challenges the conventional wisdom that meaningful participation is possible only in small groups. Yes, such groups play a vital role in our lives. I have organized them and still lead one in our home. But as the collection of examples in Chapter Six demonstrates, significant interaction can also occur in the congregation when everyone meets in the larger group—even though the dynamic differs greatly from that in a small group. When did the church buy into the idea that one-anothering, which forms the very core of Jesus's new command, must be mostly barred from larger congregational settings? To their credit, some congregations are learning to gather in ways, using a variety of approaches, that counter passivity and cultivate active discipleship.

Chapters One through Five examine the biblical basis for making church meetings participative and identify some of the traditional forces that push us toward spectatoritis. Chapter Six describes practices gleaned from more than two dozen church leaders, examples that show how they are breaking from tradition and involving the priesthood of all believers in their worship services. This long chapter, in which churches appear alphabetically, focuses on those one-anothering actions called for in the New Testament that can be practiced when we gather. For those who wish to move in this direction, Chapter Seven suggests several ways to prepare a congregation to set out on the journey to life-changing participation.

In writing these pages I have tried to practice what I am preaching by making the book itself participatory. A short epigraph introduces every chapter, each written by a separate author. The examples in Chapter Six have come from 25 different church leaders. So this is a multivoiced book calling for multivoiced church practices.

Curing Sunday Spectatoritis

This book is for all who love the Body of Christ and work for its well-being. It is for pastors, church leaders, and church planters in all kinds of communities—in urban, suburban, exurban, and rural congregations. It is for Christians who seek to encourage increased congregational participation and to support leaders as they pursue that objective. If you are or will be in a position to influence the format of church meetings, I hope you will discover one or more ideas you can adapt to your own situation. Or perhaps some of the examples will spark your thinking for creating other ways to increase participation in your main weekly meeting. If you are planting a church, the material in these chapters should help you establish ways of meeting that prevent the onset of spectatoritis. For large churches and those with decades of history, moving toward meetings that incorporate one-anothering will be more difficult—but not impossible.

Having served as a senior pastor for 21 years, I understand the pressures and joys of leadership in the gathered church. Having served as an employee and business owner for 28 years, I have experienced many of the dilemmas that confront believers in that major part of the scattered church. (Those roles overlapped during eight bivocational years.) Drawing on insights gained from my experience in the gathered and scattered church, I hope these pages may assist those who shape the way we gather in exploring how better to prepare believers "for the work people who follow Christ must do" (Eph. 4:12, UBS New Testament Handbook Series).

(Note: Chapter introductions were written specifically for this book. They have not come from previously published sources.

Each author is identified immediately following his or her epigraph.)

CHAPTER 1

Spectatoritis vs. One-Anothering

Urban followers of Christ in particular are wondering if church is relevant to the issues and pressures they are facing each day. No longer content to hear a pre-packaged message, or more generalizations, or well-worn stories, they are asking to do life together, to interact over the intersection of the gospel message and the myriad of ways that life in the city either undermines or builds their humanity. They come hoping to be more than a mere collection of disconnected individuals but a grand one-another. In this scenario, they, not the pastor alone in solitude, set the agenda, the message, the conversation over it, and the implications of it. The more participatory the better.

Dr. Randy White, Executive Director,
Fresno Pacific University Center for Community
Transformation, Fresno, CA

Spectatoritis. The term speaks for itself. No dictionary needed. Back in 1932, Jay Nash's book by that title warned that America was becoming a nation of onlookers: "The average man who has time on his hands turns out to be a spectator, a watcher of somebody else, merely because that is the easiest thing. He becomes a victim of spectatoritis."[1]

---

[1] Jay B. Nash, *Spectatoritis*, (New York: Holston House, 1932), 5.

Like arthritis, bronchitis, and appendicitis, spectatoritis brings on a measure of disability. But unlike those and other inflammatory "-itis" conditions that ache and throb, Sunday spectatoritis typically leaves its victims quite pain-free, even comfortable. And who among us, including church people, will seek a cure if unaware of any disabling symptoms?

Yet some have seen and reported on the telltale signs of disease. Decades ago a few church leaders began using the term spectatoritis to call attention to the sit-watch-and-listen format of church meetings.

Warnings from Older Voices

Twentieth-century author and theologian Elton Trueblood said: "All of us suffer from a terrible sickness in our churches. It is called Spectatoritis. . . . The secret is participation, participation, participation."[2] But in spite of his diagnosis of the disease and his prescription for its cure made long ago, the illness persists.

In 1955 into a folder with a sermon on worship, Martin Luther King, Jr. inserted an outline that included this note:

> There are many people who have caught the contagious disease of "spectatoritis." Such persons are only spectators or onlookers but not participants. Such persons watch the minister and choir indulge in prayer and praise. They come to see what is going on rather than to help create, give direction and enrichment to what is going on. The mood of the true worshiper

---

[2] Elton Trueblood, quoted in Edward F. Murphy, *The Gifts of the Spirit and the Mission of the Church* (Pasadena, CA: master's thesis, Fuller Theological Seminary, 1972), 152.

is not passive, but active. He comes not just to get but to give, not to observe, but to participate; not just to see what is going on, but to contribute to what is going on.[3]

In *The Reconstruction of the Church—On What Pattern?* E. Stanley Jones identified the trend in churches even a half-century ago:

> The very setup of the ordinary church tends to produce the anonymous. The congregation is supposed to be silent and receptive and the pastor is supposed to be outgoing and aggressive. That produces by its very makeup the spectator and the participant. By its very makeup it produces the recessive, the ingrown, the nonconributive, and the parasite. Men and women who during the week are molders of opinion, directors of large concerns, directors of destinies are expected to be putty on Sunday, and are supposed to like it. They have little responsibility, hence make little response, except, perhaps, "I enjoyed your sermon." They have little to do, hence they do little.[4]

In 1972 Ray Stedman, pastor of Peninsula Bible Church in Palo Alto, CA, published his widely read book, *Body Life*. He wrote of the "gradual transfer of responsibility from the people to what was termed 'the clergy'. . . . When the ministry was thus left to the professionals there was nothing left for the people to do other than

---

[3] The Martin Luther King, Jr., Papers Project: "Worship, Sermon at Dexter Avenue Baptist Church," accessed June 6, 2016, https://swap.stanford.edu/20141218225616/http://mlk-kpp01.stanford.edu/primarydocuments/Vol6/7Aug1955Worship.pdf (accessed June 6, 2016).

[4] E. Stanley Jones, *The Reconstruction of the Church—On What Pattern?* (Nashville: Abingdon Press, 1970), 109.

come to church and listen. . . . Soon Christianity became nothing but a spectator sport."[5]

Concern Continues in Younger Voices

Church spectating continues today. It is "viewers vs. doers" says blogger Brett McKay. He laments that spectatoritis "has seeped into all areas of our lives." That includes churches he visited: "People listened to the music, watched a video and powerpoint presentation, sat through a short message from the pastor, and left 60 minutes later. There were no requirements for participation or service of any kind. It was interesting to see that worship had become yet another thing to be passively *consumed*, as opposed to actively *created*."[6]

Another blogger, Thom Shultz, has written: "Sunday is a time for spectator sports. At the stadium. In the arena. On the field. And in the church. File in. Sit in rows. Watch the professionals perform. File out. That's the job of the spectator. Over the years, the church has drifted away from participation, toward passive spectatorship."[7]

Spectatoritis afflicts Christians internationally. Anne Wilkinson-Hayes, Acting Director of Ministries in the Baptist

---

[5] Ray Stedman, *Body Life* (Glendale, CA: Regal Books Division, G/L Publications, 1972), 78.

[6] Brett McKay, "Viewers vs. Doers: The Rise of Spectatoritis," *The Art of Manliness* (blog), August 28, 2011, accessed April 13, 2016, http://www.artofmanliness.com/2011/08/28/viewers-vs-doers-the-rise-of-spectatoritis/.

[7] Thom S. Schultz, "The Big New Spectator Sport: Church," *Holy Soup with Tom Schultz* (blog), February 3, 2011, accessed April 13, 2016, http://holysoup.com/2011/02/03/the-big-new-spectator-sport-church/.

Curing Sunday Spectatoritis

Union of Victoria, Australia, says, "I visit a lot of very different churches, and I have to say that increasingly the Sunday worship experience is a very passive affair for the majority of attendees."[8] In the UK, Peter Holmes agrees: "Part of our contemporary problem is that we are creating a culture of observers rather than a participatory culture. This only adds to our sense of isolation."[9]

Treating Sunday Spectatoritis

How can a church cure Sunday Spectatoritis? Although Trueblood, quoted above, received his doctorate in philosophy, not medicine, he wrote the prescription for the illness long ago: "participation, participation, participation." In his book, *The Incendiary Fellowship*, Trueblood elaborated on his prescription:

> There is little chance of renewal if all that we have is the arrangement by which one speaks and the others listen. One trouble with this conventional system is that the speaker never knows what the unanswered questions are, or what reservations remain in the [listener's] mentality. Somehow or other we must arrange opportunities for Christian dialogue, since the old idea of the preacher standing ten feet above contradiction simply will not do.[10]

---

[8] Sian and Stuart Murray Williams, *The Power of All: Building a Multivoiced Church* (Harrisonburg, VA: Herald Press, 2012), 9.

[9] Peter R. Holmes, *Trinity in Human Community: Exploring Congregational Life in the Image of the Social Trinity* (Bletchley, UK: Paternoster Press, 2006), 46.

[10] Elton Trueblood, *The Incendiary Fellowship* (New York: Harper & Row Publishers, Inc., 1967), 61.

Roget's Thesaurus offers just one antonym for spectator: *participant*.[11] To spectate and to participate are polar opposites. Participation can and does happen in small groups, cell groups, and house churches. It is expressed in many ways: conversations, affirmations, reservations, dialogue, questions, objections, and answers. But must that kind of involvement stay locked outside the larger gatherings most call church? Must congregations settle for the spectatoritis status quo on Sunday?

Some might say we need to return to the model of the New Testament church. In the Corinthian church, for example, Paul expected that everyone should have the opportunity to speak up (1 Cor. 14:26). Spectating must have been difficult in those meetings! Of course, gathering in houses, as the first-century church did, made participation far easier than in larger venues. The architecture, furniture, and arrangement of living rooms all invite mutual contribution.

Does the New Testament offer any carved-in-stone formula for how to structure the church or its meetings? No. As Robert Banks puts it, "[Paul's] organization of community life contains no detailed confession or code to subscribe to, no liturgical order to govern their meetings, no clerical leadership to control its affairs."[12] In this book I will not promote any ideal pattern or recommend an impossible return to the first-century church. The question is not, what is the New Testament's format-recipe for our meetings? Instead I suggest we ask, what core New Testament

---

[11] *Roget's Thesaurus*, s.v. "spectator."
[12] Robert Banks, *Paul's Idea of Community* (Peabody, MA: Hendrickson Publishers, Inc., 1994), 190.

theme should shape the meeting agenda when Christ-followers gather?

This question sends us back even further than the meeting patterns we can identify in the New Testament church. Their practices for gathering were not simply pragmatic inventions. Those first believers had good reasons for adopting the meeting formats we read about in Paul's letters. Jesus's words were fresh in their hearts and minds. From what they had seen and heard from the One they had come to know as the Way, they had learned the way to gather. So what they did when they assembled naturally traced its roots to what Jesus had said about how they should relate to each other.

The New Command

The night before his crucifixion, Jesus had a long conversation with his first disciples. In John's account of that exchange, a major theme keeps showing up: *commands*. In John 13-15 (NIV), Jesus refers to his Father's commands twice (14:31, 15:10), but he speaks of his own commands no less than seven times (13:34, 14:15, 14:21, 15:10, 15:12, 15:14, 15:17). And within this lengthy dialogue with his followers, he spells out what he calls his new command. Right after telling them he will soon be leaving for a place they cannot come, he says, "A new command I give you: Love one another. As I have loved you, so you must love one another. By this all men will know that you are my disciples, if you love one another" (John 13:34-35).

The NIV translates these verses in two English sentences totaling 27 words. As Jesus presents and explains his new command in those two sentences, he repeats "one another" three times. These "one anothers" became the seed from which grew the more than 50 one-another/each-other commands in the New Testament letters. Thus, *one-anothering* is a core New Testament principle for practicing our faith—the way we serve, the way we set our priorities, and the way we gather.

Suppose you have been sitting in a corner watching Jesus wash his disciples' feet. You have just heard him verbalize his new command. But you're puzzled. So you raise your hand and do something participatory by asking, "Excuse me for interrupting, but how is this command new? After all, the command to love others has been around for some 1500 years. Back in Moses's day, God commanded us to 'love your neighbor as yourself.' And, Jesus, you yourself have repeated and confirmed this command to love our neighbors—even calling it the second greatest commandment. So I'm finding it hard to understand. What is *new* in this new command?"

No, you weren't there to raise this question. But had you done so, I suspect Jesus might have identified the newness as lying in at least three areas.

New Recipients of the Loving

First, in the new command those who receive the love differ from those in the old command. Your neighbor in that earlier command might be a fellow believer. But life in a pluralistic culture means your neighbor—next door, at work, or elsewhere— might well be an atheist, an agnostic, or someone in a strange cult. In other words, the old love-your-neighbor command had no faith-based litmus test for identifying its beneficiaries. But the one anothers in the new command point to fellow disciples, Jesus-followers, companions on the Way. Thus, the scope of the new command is narrower and more focused than that of the old command.

New Standard for the Loving

Second, in the new command the criterion for the love differs from that in the old command. The benchmark for love in the old command was "as yourself." We all look out for number one. So the old command instructed us to seek the well-being of others just as we look out for our own. By contrast, the standard in the new command is "as I have loved you." How has Jesus loved us? John explains: "We know what real love is because Jesus gave up his life for us. So we also ought to give up our lives for our brothers and sisters" (1 John 3:16, NLT). The dozens of one-another commands in the New Testament simply spell out concrete ways of laying down our lives for each other.

New Results of the Loving

The third area of newness is actually not part of the command itself. Instead, it lies in how Jesus explained the result of obeying. If we, his followers, love each other in the self-sacrificing way he loves us, "all men will know that you are my disciples" (John 13:35). In short, the most convincing evidence to not-yet-Christians that we are apprenticed to Christ is the way we practice self-giving love for fellow apprentices.

A little later during the same evening and in the same room as they had heard this new command, the disciples listened as Jesus addressed his Father in the prayer recorded in John 17. In that prayer, he said something similar about the results of this mutual, self-giving love:

> I pray also for those who will believe in me through their message, that all of them may be one, Father, just as you are in me and I am in you. May they also be in us *so that the world may believe that you have sent me* [emphasis added]. I have given them the glory that you gave me, that they may be one as we are one: I in them and you in me. May they be brought to complete unity *to let the world know that you sent me* [emphasis added] and have loved them even as you have loved me (John 17:20-23).

To *believe* and to *know* God sent Jesus, the world needs to see demonstrations of authentic, self-emptying unity and love among believers. Nonbelievers are not seeing that kind of love and oneness. Not in their homeowner associations. Not in their governments. Not in their workplaces. And far too often, not in their families. Love and unity like that have just one source.

Trinitarian One-Anothering

One-anothering had already been established long before Jesus put his new command into words at the Last Supper. God—Father, Son, and Holy Spirit—had been one-anothering throughout eternity. Scripture consistently shows us the persons of the Trinity communicating with each other. From the plural pronouns in the conversational "let us make man in our image" (Gen. 1:26), to the Father's teaching the Son what to say (John

8:28), to the Holy Spirit's perfect understanding of God's thoughts (1 Cor. 2:11), the members of the Godhead are in continuous and harmonious dialogue. Nothing can separate them. They have been, are, and always will be joined in mutuality and reciprocity. So in our human way of speaking we might say they are always gathered. Even when Father and Son were, so to speak, scattered, when he came to earth, Jesus knew his Father was with him (John 8:29; 16:32). Father, Son, and Holy Spirit all participate in one-anothering, with each doing his own unique work. The triune God, then, is participatory, relational, dialogical—and we are made in his likeness.

This has far-reaching effects for the church and ministry. As Paul Stevens explains, "There was ministry before there was a world, ministry in the being of God. This mutual interanimation, interpenetration, indwelling, covenantal loyalty and othering—what the Cappadocian fathers in the fourth and fifth centuries called 'perichoresis'—is the mutual service rendered within God."[13]

From this, Stevens draws out three implications for "the perichoretic church":

- First, there is no such thing as an individual member.
- Second, there is no hierarchy of ministries.
- Third, all members of the laos [people] of God belong to one another, minister to one another, need one another

---

[13] R. Paul Stevens, *The Other Six Days: Vocation, Work, and Ministry in Biblical Perspective* (Grand Rapids, MI: Wm. B. Eerdmans Publishing Co., 1999), 141.

and contribute to the rich unity and ministry of the whole.[14]

In *Trinity in Human Community*, Peter R. Holmes explains how understanding God as "social Trinity" translates into church life: "Having the idea of the persons of the Trinity pouring their life into one another permanently in divine loving harmony is extremely helpful when trying to imagine how a faith community can seek, by the way it lives, to mirror the divine nature."[15]

This triune God is streaming his love and unity—by his very own Spirit—into the Church. Now it is up to us to preserve these gifts in our practice. We need to pattern our gatherings after the divine assembly. Here on earth, by the way we meet together and live out one-anothering, we show the world that we are drawing from the only source of unity and completely-for-each-other love in the universe. One-anothering in our church relationships is, above all, a powerful way to reflect the fact that we are made in the likeness of our Father who sent his Son into our world. This makes one-anothering the most potent basis for evangelism.

One-Anothering and the Great Commission

Some have said nothing should trump the Great Commission. Matthew's Gospel ends with Jesus saying, "Therefore go and make disciples of all nations, baptizing them in the name of the Father and of the Son and of the Holy Spirit, and teaching

---

[14] Ibid, 63-64.
[15] Holmes, *Trinity in Human Community,* 38.

them to obey everything I have commanded you. And surely I am with you always, to the very end of the age" (Matt. 28:19-20).

Would an emphasis on practicing one-anothering when we meet distract us from focusing on what we should *really* be doing? Are participatory church meetings simply an ingrown, we-centered way to escape the main priority of Jesus?

Three action-items make up the heart of the Great Commission: disciple-making, baptizing, and teaching. The latter two expand on the first by detailing how disciple-making is to be done. After new believers are incorporated into the body of Christ through baptism, they are to receive teaching. And the teaching is to cover everything Jesus commanded.

Surely what Jesus went out of his way to call his new command must head the list of those things he commanded his initial disciples to do. Obeying what he calls us to do demonstrates our love for him: "If you love me, you will obey what I command" (John 14:15). Because his new command calls us to love one another, we reveal our love for Jesus in the way we love each other. We might paraphrase John 14:15 this way: If you love me, you will practice one-anothering.

The timing of his giving the new command is significant—during their last meal together, just before Jesus's crucifixion. He had gone to extra lengths to arrange a just-right setting. Just as you and I would if we knew we were going to eat together for a final time, he chose his words carefully. In case those first-generation disciples (or we later ones) might have missed his point, Jesus repeated the essence of his new command twice more that same evening: "My command is this: Love each other as I have loved you" (John 15:12). And, "This is my command: Love each other" (John 15:17).

As we have already seen, he did not simply recycle the Old Covenant commandment about loving our neighbors. The fresh content of the New Covenant command must have had such priority in his thinking that a mere replay of the old one would not do. In stating the new command, he put one-anothering among his followers at the top of our to-do list. Our obedience to it authenticates to unbelievers our claim to be followers of Jesus. So the Great Commission itself underscores the urgency for contemporary church leaders to teach Jesus's apprentices to obey him by one-anothering.

The most effective teaching involves far more than simply telling learners what to do. It also means providing them with opportunities to practice actually carrying out the instructions. So whenever the Church gathers, a major part of teaching believers to obey all that Jesus commanded will be to structure the meeting in such a way that they can, as apprentices must, experience doing those commands. Which brings us back to Elton Trueblood's antidote for spectatoritis: "participation, participation, participation." But meetings in which believers mainly sit, watch, and listen provide precious little opportunity to carry out what Jesus calls for in his new command.

One-Anothering as the Reason for Gathering

The New Testament does not specifically say to meet with one another in exactly those terms. But the many *together* words leave no doubt that this is God's design for his church. We read about the Church coming together, meeting together, joining together, eating together, and conferring together. Hebrews 10:24 and 25 warn against *not* meeting together—church dropouts were apparently a problem even back then. But these verses explain—in one-anothering terms—the purpose for meeting together. According to this passage, the downside of not meeting together has nothing to do with missing the opportunity to worship. The danger is not that believers would lose out on hearing sermons. Instead, if believers do not keep meeting together, they will not be able to "spur one another on to love and good deeds" (Heb. 10:24) and to "encourage one another" (Heb. 10:25). We are to do this kind of one-anothering "all the more as you see the Day approaching" (Heb. 10:25).

What makes gathering for mutual nudging on so essential? Why must we pick up the pace as the end times draw nearer? Jesus warned that "because of the increase of wickedness, the love of most will grow cold" (Matt. 24:12). The progress of evil in the last days, he said, will freeze out the capacity of most people to love. Because the environment we live in chills lived-out love in each of us, we need to keep on meeting together and, when we do, to "spur one another on to love" and to the good works that flow from it.

Further, all of us are vulnerable to the power of sin to overtake us and calcify our hearts. Jesus himself asked a haunting question: "When the Son of Man comes, will he find faith on the earth?" (Luke 18:8). So when we gather, we must "encourage one another" (Heb. 3:13), not just now and then—with summers off— but often.

Participatory Gathering Meets a Roadblock

But a high wall hampers one-anothering and participation in our main congregational gatherings: a wall built brick by brick from church traditions. Traditions can be helpful, neutral, or harmful. In its era, the Jewish synagogue was a helpful tradition. Although God had not prescribed synagogues in the Torah (they originated during the exile), by the time Jesus walked on earth they had become a helpful custom in which he regularly participated. But he strongly opposed hurtful human traditions, such as the practice of the religious Jews who justified not supporting parents by saying that what they might have provided for Dad and Mom had been earmarked for God (Mark 7:11-13).

Jesus leveled some of his harshest words against man-made religious traditions that had become more significant than directives from his Father. In doing so, he reflected for his own contemporaries the denunciations God had spoken against their ancestors through the Old Covenant prophets. Yes, God had commanded his people to assemble (e.g., Num. 8:9; Deut. 31:12). But his instructions had been displaced by their own ways of doing things—their humanly devised traditions—to the point where their gatherings and religious practices disgusted him. *The Message* paraphrase vividly captures his displeasure: "Quit your worship charades. I can't stand your trivial religious games: Monthly conferences, weekly Sabbaths, special meetings—meetings, meetings, meetings—I can't stand one more! Meetings for this, meetings for that. I hate them! You've worn me out!" (Isa. 1:13-14, MSG). "I can't stand your religious meetings. . . . I've had all I can take of your noisy ego-music" (Amos 5:21, 23, MSG).

Curing Sunday Spectatoritis

Over the past two millennia the Church has had plenty of time to develop its own humanly invented hand-me-downs that shape the way we assemble. One generation inserts this routine, the next generation attaches that custom. Each add-on seems to make perfect sense at the time it is appended. As these practices accumulate and age, they become highly esteemed and seemingly indispensable. The next chapter will explore some of our contemporary church meeting traditions that, while perhaps helpful in some ways, typically interfere with participation and one-anothering.

CHAPTER 2

Meetings Shaped by Tradition

Today, many churches have focused on developing into microcosms of corporate culture. This "corporate" culture places considerable emphasis on church membership (numbers), activities, reputation, status and visibility. In essence, the church itself becomes a market of worship experiences that one chooses according to the church's rating, reputation or popularity. However, as the Church shifts its emphasis on external outputs, it loses its sight on edifying, encouraging and promoting the spiritual growth of believers, the church eventually loses its effectiveness. Church attendance may grow, but how many are being discipled? "What good is salt if salt loses its saltiness, how can it be made salty again?" (Matthew 5:13, NIV). Is the present state of our inner city communities evidence of the effectiveness of our churches? Have some churches lost their saltiness?

Dr. Stanley A. Holbrook,
First Baptist Church of Penn Hills,
Pittsburgh, PA

"McDonaldization." Yes, it is a word now showing up in online dictionaries. The term comes from sociologist George Ritzer's book, *The McDonaldization of Society*. To earn my way through Wheaton College in Illinois, I worked in one of the first McDonald's restaurants located in the neighboring town of Glen Ellyn. My boss, using electronic probes in potatoes, pioneered those now-famous French fries. I learned to load burger patties

35

onto a framework that could drop 36 of them onto the grill all at once. During my time there, we changed the sign under the yellow arch to read "We have sold over 1 million." So I was able to watch as the company developed the systems which turned into the traditions that eventually helped it grow to 36,000-plus restaurants in more than 100 countries around the world.[1]

Characteristics of McDonaldization

In his book, Ritzer identified four characteristics of McDonaldization.

Efficiency.

How do you get the most meals to the most people with the least amount of cost, effort, and time? Not for nothing is McDonald's known as a fast food chain.

Calculability.

The most important things are measurable. How many burgers, fries, and shakes have been sold? How much time elapsed from taking orders to serving food? How much profit was realized?

Predictability.

Your taste buds should not be able to tell the difference between the Big Mac you purchase in New York and one you order in California. McDonald's caters to the fact that millions of people want to live in an unsurprising world.

Control.

---

[1] "Our Story," McDonald's Corporation, accessed January 23, 2016, http://www.mcdonalds.com/us/en/our_story.html.

By making certain things automatic (rather than leaving them up to the abilities and judgment of workers), that is, by "de-skilling" employees, management gains more control. By design, employees do only "a limited number of things."[2]

McDonaldization in the Church

Although the McDonald's fast-food chain was born in the U.S., it was Britain's John Drane who saw ecclesiastical parallels and described them in *The McDonaldization of the Church*. In Chapter 19 of another book by Ritzer, *McDonaldization: The Reader*, Drane explains why he wrote his own book: "It soon became evident that McDonaldization . . . did indeed describe the way that many people experience the church, even if they are not values that all church leaders would self-consciously espouse as their guiding principles."[3] Consider a few examples of how the guiding principles of McDonaldization seem to have influenced the way we do church.

Efficiency.

For instance, take the Lord's Supper, which began as a real meal, a participatory occasion with dialogue and one-anothering. In the John 13-15 account of the Passover meal, the disciples interact with Jesus and each other, commenting or asking questions more than a dozen times. But meals take time. So the menu has been reduced to one we can finish in, say, ten minutes.

---

[2] George F. Ritzer, *The McDonaldization of Society* (New York, NY: Sage Publications, Inc., 2007), 15.
[3] George F. Ritzer, *McDonaldization: The Reader* (New York, NY: Sage Publications, Inc., 2009), 222.

Like every other element in the meeting, this must fit into the time slot predetermined for the weekly get-together. As a result, one-anothering has been cropped from the original table-gathering picture. Customary Communion words, mostly the same each time and spoken only by the one officiating, have replaced what was at first back-and-forth table talk.

Calculability.

Drane illustrates this tendency in church life by recalling a conversation he had with the pastor of a U.S. megachurch: "He had been forced to adopt a ministry style which was 'geared towards filling the building, instead of filling the people.' He had started with just seventeen people, and ended up with more than 3000, but in the process the church had become a depersonalized machine."[4]

Many denominational conferences for pastors leave no doubt that filling the building does matter. Bodies, budgets, and buildings are relatively easy to measure and can become the de facto signs of success. In describing how churches fit their Sunday meetings into precut time slots, Drane says: "Because of our commitment to this kind of time calculability, many of our churches are simply not geared up to spend time either to explore God or to make meaningful connections with other Christians."[5]

Predictability.

---

[4] John Drane, *The McDonaldization of the Church: Consumer Culture and the Church's Future* (Macon, GA: Smyth & Helwys Publishing, Incorporated, 2001), 45.
[5] Ibid., 48.

In many churches the sequence has become so repetitive that regulars do not even have to look at the order of service printed in the bulletin to know what is coming next. To some church regulars it feels as if they are attending the same church meeting over and over again. This, says Drane, "is both a strength and a weakness. The security of what is predictable can indeed help people feel safe—but the downside is that it all becomes routine."[6]

Control.

"The issue of power and control is at the heart of all the other factors that are at work in a McDonaldized style of being,"[7] says Drane. In a church meeting, professionals decide what will and will not take place. Spontaneous use of gifts by those in the audience would leave room for mistakes and divergent views. Those allowed to make announcements from the platform may preface what they say with something like, I've been given three minutes for this. Various factors explain this precision: relieving nursery workers at a certain time, making way for a tandem meeting scheduled soon afterward, or fitting into the time slot for a recording or TV program.

Like McDonald's, churches over the centuries have developed systems that in time became traditions. By replicating these ecclesiastical customs, the church has multiplied into what came to be called Christendom. Those traditions help explain why, when I visited a Three-Self Church in Xian, China, it felt—except

---

[6] Ibid.
[7] Ibid., 54.

for the language—just like sitting in a church service in the United States some four or five decades ago. Many ecclesiastical systems, seen as useful when they were first developed, have been franchised and exported, surviving long after their pull dates. Yet they continue to exert their sway over the way we structure our church meetings.

What Forces Shape Our Gatherings?

Bread comes in all sorts of forms: loaf, roll, crumpet, bagel, focaccia, flatbread, and on it goes. As simple and commonplace as it is, bread takes on its shape through the application of various forces. A baker's hands (or machines these days) knead and divide the dough. Working from the inside, yeast, baking powder, or sourdough starter makes it rise. Working from the outside, a pan or tray forms the bottom or sides. Gravity exerts its own pressure on the dough as well. As we savor the texture and flavor of a mouthful of bread, we seldom, if ever, think about the pressures that shaped it.

In a similar way, when we gather with other Christians, we rarely consider the forces that are shaping the "dough" of our meetings. But whether we recognize them or not, certain traditional templates largely shape the contours of the way we assemble. A great many of them began centuries ago but still exert enormous pressure. Others came along more recently. Certain traditions can work something like gyroscopes on a ship, helping us to maintain our balance. But too many, like quicksand, can mire us down and immobilize us. The body of Christ and the body of church traditions have become so conjoined that separating them requires delicate surgery.

The rest of this chapter will focus on how certain customary ways of thinking about and doing church inhibit one-anothering. One is the notion that our main reason for gathering is to worship.

The Worship Maxim

What do nearly all churches and Christians take as a given for why we gather? *Worship.* The meeting itself is almost always referred to as the *worship service.* Those who direct singing are called *worship leaders,* usually surrounded by *worship teams.* We describe our hymns and choruses as *worship and praise songs* (triggers for what some have called *worship wars*). Sometimes the meeting place itself is called the *worship center.* Today, churches can buy *worship videos.* At least one church has a designated *worship producer.* In each case just cited, worship, as an adjective, modifies something associated with a church meeting. However, in the New Testament, the word worship is never used in this way.

Naturally, if church leaders see worship as the predominant purpose of Christians assembling, that vision will become the framework they use for shaping the agenda to make that happen in the meeting. Typically, it is assumed that specialists or leaders need to create a worshipful atmosphere. This is done through a carefully designed program by which the congregation is taken through a preplanned sequence intended to inspire reverence for and devotion to God.

Curing Sunday Spectatoritis

One web page asks why we gather to worship. It includes these words in its answer: "Worship is a time for showing our love for God, for being with God, and for breathing in the goodness, mercy, and beauty of God."[8] Another website offers "34 Tips for Creating Powerful Worship Experiences and Vibrant Worship Teams."[9] A mindset like that in the latter example can turn worship into an experience leaders devise ahead of time and produce for a congregation.

In response to Thom S. Rainier's blog post, "Should Your Church Stop Having a Stand and Greet Time?" one reader explained emphatically why a greeting should have no place in the congregational meeting: "You do that before and after worship — not DURING worship! Worship is for God – that is why you are there!!!"[10] Indeed, worship is one of those elements that should be preserved in meeting together as we have known it. Worship should characterize our lives when we are gathered as well as when we are scattered. Our hearts should soar toward heaven as we hear again the story of God's redemptive love poured out through his Son, Jesus Christ. And the adoration that arises in us when we sing of God's amazing grace is certainly pleasing to him.

---

[8] MennoMedia, "The Heart of Mennonite Worship: Five Vital Rhythms," MennoMedia, accessed April 15, 2016, http://www.mpn.net/worship/pdf/HoMW_1.pdf.

[9] Matt Tullos, "34 Tips for Creating Powerful Worship Experiences and Vibrant Worship Teams," *Louisiana Baptists* (blog), accessed April 15, 2016, https://louisianabaptists.org/34-tips-for-creating-powerful-worship-experiences-and-vibrant-worship-teams/.

[10] Ken, November 24, 2014, comment on Thom S. Rainier, "Should Your Church Stop Having a Stand and Greet Time?," *Thom S. Rainer* (blog), November 3, 2014, http://thomrainer.com/2014/11/church-stop-stand-greet-time/.

Why Should We Gather?

But there is more to be said here. It may seem heretical to question this long-standing tradition of making worship the main reason for our gathering. However, after thoroughly studying the relevant New Testament passages, theologian I. Howard Marshall came to a different conclusion. In an article entitled "How Far Did the Early Christians Worship God?" he writes: "Our examination of the NT evidence has shown quite conclusively that worship strictly so called was only one feature of the Christian meeting. . . . To speak of a Christian meeting as being 'a service of worship' with the implication that everything which takes place must somehow be related directly to this primary purpose is to depart seriously from the NT pattern."[11]

Marshall shows that the New Testament reason for gathering as the church can be pictured as a dynamic movement along the lines of a triangle.

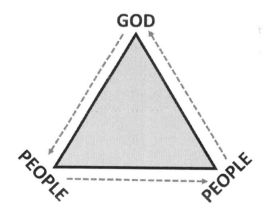

---

[11] I. Howard Marshall, "How Far Did the Early Christians Worship God?," accessed April 15, 2016, http://churchsociety.org/docs/churchman/099/Cman_099_3_Marshall.pdf.

He explains the "flow" represented by the triangle this way:

When a specific function or purpose is ascribed to a church meeting [in the New Testament] it is not the glorification of God but the building up of the church and the ministry to its members. *Church meetings are for the benefit of the congregation and so indirectly for the glory of God* [emphasis added]. Worship in the sense of giving praise to God is thus logically secondary to ministry in the sense of God's ministry to us. At the same time, since this ministry is exercised between persons, the church meeting has the character of fellowship in which the keynote is mutual love. The symbol of the church, therefore, is not simply an upward arrow from man to God, nor simply a downward arrow from God to man, but rather a triangle representing the lines of *grace coming down from God to his people, the flow of grace from person to person, and the response of thanks and petition to God* [emphasis added].[12]

That last phrase, "the response of thanks and petition to God," makes it clear Marshall does believe worship has a place in our church meetings. But it is not the primary New Testament reason for gathering. Instead, he is saying that when believers, together, experience the grace of God and are given the opportunity to serve each other with their grace-gifts, the result is a spontaneous upsurge of worship.

Glance again at the words from the website quoted earlier: "Worship is a time for showing our love for God, for being with God, and for breathing in the goodness, mercy, and beauty of

---

[12] Ibid.

God." Where, in this statement, is any focus on our ministry to our fellow believers who have gathered with us? Even when all alone, any of us can show our love for God, be with him, and breathe in his goodness, mercy, and beauty. But if we are to build, strengthen, and encourage each other, we need to get together. On the basis of his study of the New Testament, Marshall makes the point that "the main emphasis in church meetings lay upon what the members did for one another in virtue of their charismatic endowment from God."[13] In Ephesians 4:12 and 16, Paul makes it clear that God's people are to do their "works of service" to build each other up, and that the body "grows and builds itself up in love as each part does its work." From these and other passages, Marshall says, "the function of church meetings and the activities which take place in them are now clearly seen to be directed towards the congregation itself and only indirectly towards God."[14]

Other Voices on Why We Meet

Marshall is not the only Bible scholar who has noticed the difference between our traditional emphasis on worship as the reason for gathering and what the New Testament actually says. In *Paul's Idea of Community*, Robert Banks writes:

> One of the most puzzling features of Paul's understanding of *ekklesia* for his contemporaries, whether Jews or Gentiles, must have been his failure to say that a person went to church primarily to "worship." Not once in all his writings does he suggest that this is the case. Indeed it could not be, for he

---

[13] Ibid., 5.
[14] Ibid., 6.

held a view of "worship" that prevented him from doing so . . . Worship involves the whole of one's life, every word and action, and knows no special place or time. . . . Since all places and times have now become the venue for worship, Paul cannot speak of Christians assembling in church distinctively for this purpose. They are already worshipping God, acceptably or unacceptably, in whatever they are doing. While this means that when they are in church they are worshipping as well, it is not worship but something else that marks off their coming together from everything else that they are doing.[15]

Banks explains that "something else" like this: "The purpose of the church is the growth and edification of its members into Christ and into a more common life through their God-given ministry to one another."[16]

In *The Priesthood of All Believers*, Milt Rodriguez writes,

Even though worship is very important, we must realize that worship is not the reason we gather together. Paul teaches that worship is offering up our whole lives to God (see Rom. 12:1, 2). We don't come together primarily to worship because our whole life is to be an act of worship. . . . So what *is* the main purpose for us to gather together as believers? *It is for the purpose of edification of the members through their God-given ministry to one another.*[17]

---

[15] Banks, *Paul's Idea of Community*, 88-89.

[16] Ibid., 90.

[17] Milt Rodriguez, *The Priesthood of All Believers: 1st Century Church Life in the 21st Century* (The Rebuilders, 2004), 106.

His study of the New Testament led David Norrington to the same conclusion: "The early church was not primarily concerned with worship in its meetings. The major emphasis was on activities directed toward members of the congregation for their mutual growth and upbuilding, although worship was involved here as in every other sphere of life."[18]

The traditional idea that our gatherings are primarily for worship stands in the way of the one-anothering Jesus called for in his new command and of meeting together after the pattern seen in such passages as 1 Corinthians 14:26 and Hebrews 10:24-25. If we believe that all the attention should be directed toward God and not toward fellow believers, such things as mutual encouragement, spurring on, asking questions, and so on will be seen as interruptions that distract from our real purpose.

By contrast, leaders who see mutual upbuilding and encouragement as the central purpose of gathering will shape church meetings that open up opportunities for believers to minister to each other. Corporate worship, then, will not come about as a product of human engineering. Instead, its gracious impulse will begin in God himself, flow by his Spirit into and through his people in one-anothering, and return as faith, praise, and obedience to him.

---

[18] David C. Norrington, *To Preach or Not to Preach? The Church's Urgent Question* (Omaha, NE: Ekklesia Press, 1996), 89.

The Architectural Effect

"We shape our buildings and afterwards our buildings shape us."[19] So said Winston Churchill in a speech to the House of Commons. His observation certainly holds true for our church buildings.

While it is true that the Church met in homes for the first few centuries, the church buildings of our day do offer several advantages. Anyone who has (as I have) pulled equipment out of a closet or trailer and set up chairs to prepare for meeting in a school or rented hall, only to do the reverse after the meeting, knows how convenient a church-owned building can be. A building can accommodate a far larger group than will fit inside a home. So if a congregation wants to invite the public to an event, the building can serve that purpose well. It can house a library, provide office space, and make the church's presence visible to passersby. The typical church building has not only a main meeting room but also classrooms that work well for smaller gatherings. But in addition to these positive benefits, church buildings tend to apply powerful negative pressures that can thwart one-anothering for those meeting inside them.

Church or Theater?

In one recent weekend, my wife and I attended both a concert in a large hall in Seattle and a college graduation held in a

---

[19] "Churchill and the Commons Chamber," UK Parliament, accessed April 15, 2016, http://www.parliament.uk/about/living-heritage/building/palace/architecture/palacestructure/churchill/.

massive church building a few miles away. For me, the juxtaposition of these two events highlighted the similarities between the two venues. Each had been designed as a theater. A large, raised stage. Seats all facing the platform. Banks of spotlights. Microphones. Mixing boards. Expensive speaker systems. Each meeting space was designed to meet the needs of an audience. The New Testament speaks of the Church as a body and a family but never as an audience.

In the U. S., changes occurring in the nineteenth century pushed a shift to the playhouse model for church meeting places. That is the point made by Jeanne Halgren Kilde in her book, *When Church Became Theatre*. In 1886 the First Baptist Church of Minneapolis, MN, dedicated its new building. Indoors its features included "an elaborate stage elevated some three feet above the main floor. The term *stage* was truly an appropriate one, for the room was arranged more like a theatre or opera house than a church of previous generations."[20]

Not surprisingly, the changes in church architecture produced changes in church practice. As Kilde points out, "the same amphitheatre features that made manifest the corporate body also encouraged audiences to remain quiet and passive as they focused their attention on the stage. The theatrical spaces equated services with entertainment."[21]

---

[20] Jeanne Halgren. Kilde, *When Church Became Theater: The Transformation of Evangelical Architecture and Worship in Nineteenth-Century America* (New York: Oxford University Press, 2002), 6.
[21] Ibid., 199.

Curing Sunday Spectatoritis

Kilde shows how the trend that began in the nineteenth century came into full bloom in the megachurch buildings of the twentieth:

> They provide a space, time, and place in which one might get away from it all. Attending a service is an activity akin to going to a movie: One need not dress up, worry about the kids misbehaving, or be upset by a depressing message. . . . Just as in the late nineteenth century, hundreds of congregations, building new churches in the newest ring of suburbs now quite distant from their urban centers, now choose the amphitheatre form.[22]

By patterning our church meeting places after theaters, we squeeze the body/family into audience mode. The traditional church pew makes the squeezing literal. Latecomers often find those prime aisle spots already filled with bodies or marked as reserved with Bibles, coats, or purses. It is almost painful to watch as late arrivals scrape past knees and do tippy-toe dances to avoid stepping on shoes. For many people, only pews make them feel like they are "in church."

Yet, although church buildings began appearing around the fourth century, pews did not show up until centuries later. As David Norrington points out in *To Preach or Not to Preach?*, "in northern Europe, benches and later pews, were introduced from about the 13th century onwards. These changes may have reduced fellowship among church members still further."[23] Even the word *pew*, related to *podium*, apparently traces back to theaters.

---

[22] Ibid., 219.
[23] Norrington, *To Preach or Not to Preach?*, 58.

Today, of course, many churches provide individual chairs rather than pews. This increases the potential flexibility of the seating arrangement. But for the most part, the chairs are set up in ranks and rows like cans on a supermarket shelf. As Jeremy Thomson has noted, "it is somewhat ironic that many churches have replaced pews with chairs and yet rarely take advantage of their movability during services."[24] Unless you are sitting in the front row, the view is one of bald heads, hairdos, and the occasional face of a bored toddler peering over a parental shoulder. If the tall person in the row ahead shifts position, you must, like a bobblehead doll, keep dodging left or right to maintain a line of sight to the speaker on the platform.

Swiss theologian Eduard Schweizer expressed in *Neotestamentica* more than a half-century ago why church as theatre troubled him:

> The togetherness of the church and its services is not that of a theatre audience, where one or several paid actors act on the stage while everyone else is looking on. Each one takes part with his special gift . . . the body of Christ is not a body of soldiers in which one sees at best the neck of the preceding person . . . it is a body consisting of members living in their mutual addressing, asking, challenging, comforting, sharing of Christ and his gifts.[25]

---

[24] Jeremy Thomson, *Preaching as Dialogue: Is the Sermon a Sacred Cow?* (Cambridge, MA: Grove Books Limited, 2003), 24.

[25] Eduard Schweizer, *Neotestamentica,* (1963), quoted in Robert and Julia Banks, *The Church Comes Home* (Peabody, MA: Hendrickson Publishers, Inc., 1998), 29.

What Theaters Foster

Theaters invite performance. The October-November 1900 issue of Union Seminary Magazine included an article entitled "The Decline of the Pulpit" by Thomas R. English. He wrote: "Newspapers speak of 'pulpit performances' and 'pulpit stars' just as they do of the theatre."[26] In 1938, the Pittsburgh Post-Gazette put this headline over a story: "Pulpit Path to Stardom: Radio Celebrities Trace Ancestry to Church."[27]

It is a long-recognized reality that the elevated stage or platform provides the ideal place for star-making. Those who regularly appear up there get magnified larger than life. In a theater, only a tiny fraction of those present have platform privileges. This entitlement makes them seem more momentous than those in the audience. In the Church, any perception of nonsignificance flies directly in the face of what the New Testament teaches about the vital importance of every member of the body.

Theaters induce applause. Today, church audiences clap approval when they relate strongly with the message or music. But human adulation easily stimulates an appetite for more, and

---

[26] Thomas R. English, "The Decline of the Pulpit." *The Union Seminary Magazine 12, (*October/November 1900),, accessed April 15, 2016 https://books.google.co.in/books?id=KQEaAAAAYAAJ&pg=PA307&lpg=PA307&dq=%22pulpit+stars%22&source=bl&ots=Kn3Lr2IQIV&sig=rg-hbAVVKzutEj2KNw70EIvBWIw&hl=en&sa=X&redir_esc=y#v=onepage&q=%22pulpit%20stars%22&f=false (accessed April 15, 2016).

[27] "Pulpit Path to Stardom," *Pittsburgh Post-Gazette,* July 3, 1938, accessed April 15, 2016, https://news.google.com/newspapers?nid=1144&dat=19380703&id=ZisbAAAAIBAJ&sjid=BE0EAAAAIBAJ&pg=5835,5856598&hl=en (accessed April 15, 2016).

repeated exposure to such ovations can play havoc with the ego of those on stage. (I write this as one who served for two decades as a pastor.) Again and again, we have witnessed the elevation of Christian celebrities—whether pastors or musicians—and watched in sorrow as they fell from their lofty heights. In reality, these superstars share the weaknesses common to us all. Hero worship edifies no one.

Theaters inhibit participation. Think back to the last movie you saw in a cinema. Or to those occasions when you have attended a concert in an auditorium. Or listened to a lecture in a hall. Other than clapping (and perhaps laughing or crying), how much did you participate? Almost all the action that mattered took place up front. A good audience knows how to be reactive, mostly silent, and passive. Everyone but those on the platform or stage are expected to play the observer role.

Naturally, there are times when we should gather, facing forward, to hear someone speak. One such occasion seems to have taken place when Paul spoke to the church in Troas while the members gathered in an upstairs room—apparently the same room they used for breaking bread together (Acts 20:7-12). Even here, though, the Greek verb used to describe Paul's speaking to them is the word from which we get our word *dialogue*. Temporarily, Paul also used a lecture hall belonging to someone named Tyrannus, but the same verb indicates that he held discussions rather than presenting monologues. This may have been a large hall, but nothing suggests the church regularly met in it (Acts 19:9, 10). As Robert Banks says, in Paul's letters "the most general form of meeting . . . centered around the eating of a meal and the exercise of ministry for each other's benefit."[28]

A March 6, 2015, blog post entitled "If form follows function, perhaps we need to redesign our churches" asked some important questions:

> How can we focus on one-anothering if we are seated in rows, gazing on the backs of one another's heads? How will we confess our sins to one another, pray for one another, encourage and build one another up if we sit silently facing a stage? How do we empower all of God's people to be actively involved in one-anothering if we only give a small minority a voice, a platform, a position? Perhaps we need to rethink our spaces, rearrange our seating, and redesign our buildings to reflect the purpose and function of gathering together as a church community.[29]

Audience mode makes it very difficult for people to get to know each other. But that is the only church countless Christians have ever known and still experience week after week.

The Liturgical Lockstep

We often associate the term *liturgy* with churches traditionally considered high church. But if we understand liturgy as the order of service, the usual set of activities and the sequence in which they occur, nonliturgical—and even many house—

---

[28] Banks, *Paul's Idea of Community*, 90.

[29] Kathleen Ward, "If Form Follows Function, Perhaps We Need to Redesign Our Churches," *Church in a Circle* (blog), March 6, 2015, accessed April 15, 2016, http://www.churchinacircle.com/2015/03/06/if-form-follows-function-perhaps-we-need-to-redesign-our-churches/.

churches follow liturgies Sunday after Sunday. Here is one
example of how a liturgy flows in some churches:

Prelude

Call to Worship

Hymn

Prayer of Invocation

Prayer of Confession

Time of Silent Prayer

Assurance of Pardon

Anthem

Word to the Children

Scripture Reading

Sermon

Hymn

Offering and Offertory

Doxology

Announcements

Joys and Concerns of the Congregation

Pastoral Prayer

Lord's Prayer

Hymn

Benediction

Postlude

At first glance, this meeting agenda may seem to include
participation. For instance, there is a time for Joys and Concerns
of the Congregation. In theory, this might translate into an
opportunity for members of the body to voice their own joys and
concerns. Too often, though, they will be kept silent by being

asked to write their praises and prayer requests on cards that the pastor reads out loud to the congregation. In the liturgy shown above, the people participate in the singing of three hymns. Do they participate in choosing any songs? Or are the selections always made ahead of time by someone on their behalf?

If every word, sung or spoken, that comes from the mouths of those in the congregation has been prewritten for them, how will they learn to express their faith in their own voices? As Jeremy Thomson puts it, "it is as people have the opportunity to put their own words together that they become conscious of their thoughts and realize new paths of behavior."[30] After believers leave a church gathering for their neighborhoods and workplaces, we expect them both to demonstrate and to vocalize the gospel. But if the format of our church meetings renders them silent week after week, year after year, we have not provided them with the opportunity to develop a link between their faith and their voices.

Because a liturgy is merely a tool, it may be used in ways that incorporate one-anothering. Sian and Stuart Murray Williams explain how a liturgy can actually enhance congregational participation:

> A familiar liturgical framework may provide an ideal context for multivoiced worship. It is important that we do not equate multivoiced worship with absence of structure in our gatherings. Most communities do in fact develop a liturgical structure, even if this is not explicit or acknowledged, so a liturgical framework that is understood and valued is generally more helpful. . . .What matters is that the community

---

[30] Thomson, *Preaching as Dialogue,* 22.

understands the structure and learns how multivoiced elements relate to this.[31]

On the other hand a liturgy, as so often employed, can foster spectatoritis. The following paragraphs suggest some positives and negatives for what I am calling a "conventional" liturgy. By that I mean a liturgy generally constructed so that all elements of the meeting are preplanned, in which the voices heard are prearranged, and in which any words spoken or sung by members of the congregation are preselected by someone else and provided for them.

The Case for Conventional Liturgy

A liturgy, even if not prescribed by the traditions of a particular denomination, can offer several pluses. Among other advantages, a predefined and repeatable agenda:

Makes it easier to plan the meeting.

If one person is responsible for the content of every meeting, imagine the work it would take to come up with a fresh outline each week. But once a set sequence is adopted, planning the meeting is mostly a matter of plugging in various Scripture readings, hymns or choruses, choir numbers, and so on.

Prevents unsettling surprises.

---

[31] Sian and Stuart Murray Williams, *The Power of All: Building a Multivoiced Church.* (Harrisburg, VA: Herald Press, 2012), 83.

Meetings in which anyone might suggest a song or contribute a comment are highly unpredictable. They can even get "messy." A liturgy helps keep a lid on things.

Fits into an allotted time frame.

If it is important for the meeting to begin and end within minutes of a certain time, then a liturgy can help make that happen. In some churches, guest speakers are instructed to keep the sermon to within minutes of the time earmarked for it.

Lends itself to establishing a theme for the entire meeting.

If the sermon will be on Christ's resurrection, then the music, Scripture, and children's message can all be arranged around that topic.

Assures inclusion of important elements.

If there were no regular sequence of events, vital elements—such as prayer and Scripture reading—might be overlooked. A completely unstructured meeting could easily get lopsided.

The Case against Conventional Liturgy

On the other hand, as typically employed, a preset liturgy can also carry disadvantages. For example, it:

Can overemphasize central planning.

Typically the elements that go into a liturgy are predetermined by one or two people, likely the pastor. However, as with any Christian, the leader's knowledge and experience is limited (1 Cor. 13:9). So if the vision that is communicated and the content of the meetings are planned by the same person week in and week out, the meeting will be restricted to what the liturgy planner sees as beneficial.

Tends to create a silent majority.

Any significant interruption to the preplanned flow of the meeting is seen as a faux pas—akin to having your cell phone sound off in a crowded theater during a movie. Therefore, the last thing those who have been conditioned by a conventional liturgy want to do is say anything out loud during a church meeting. Any utterances from the members of the body—whether speaking or singing—are drafted by someone else on their behalf. Anyone able to read the PowerPoint slides on a screen can repeat the words along with everyone else. Most of the actions and words are provided for the congregation—stand up, sit down, sing this, say that. As usually employed, the liturgy blocks the opportunity for members of the body to serve one another spontaneously, speaking the truth in love, from the prompting of the Spirit within them.

Easily becomes predictable and routine—which dulls the cutting edge.

As one blogger puts it: "Routines are convenient and make for a comfortable, easy life. They make you think less. They let you predict the future. In essence, routines make you lazy. They make your life and you boring. Routines won't provide you with stories to tell.[32]

---

[32] Connie Biesalski, A Life of Blue, "The Less Routine, the More Life: How to Kill Monotony," *A Life of Blue* (blog), accessed April 18, 2016, http://www.alifeofblue.com/routine/.

Curing Sunday Spectatoritis

In some churches, video-recording the enactment of the liturgy contributes a significant shaping influence. In this way the sights and sounds can later be used in a TV broadcast or made available on the church website. This practice molds the meeting in at least these ways:

- Such recording adds pressure to plan precisely the order of events so the entire meeting will fit into the available time slot. What should have been done slowly may instead have to be rushed through.

- Making a playback copy changes the character of the meeting itself. The gathering now becomes a show or a program to produce. Things must look professional.

- The presence of the recording equipment, whether to a large or small degree, affects the way those on camera will present themselves. They are now conscious not only of those who have come together but also of an unseen audience they will probably never meet.

In *Church Refugees*, Josh Packard and Ashleigh Hope quote Mark, one of the people they interviewed for the book. He said, "The problem is that they've taken . . . order and routine and applied it to absolutely everything. It's like everything has become liturgy. It's all routine. And a lot of people need that, but there has to be room for me, too. I mean, shouldn't there also be room for me in the church?"[33]

---

[33] Josh Packard and Cynthia Hope, *Church Refugees: Sociologists Reveal Why People Are DONE With Church but Not Their Faith* (Loveland, CO: Group Publishing, 2015), 129.

The Leadership Focus

Do New Testament writers speak about church leadership? Yes. Do they give leadership the same prominence seen so often in contemporary church practice? No. In the NIV version of the New Testament letters, the word *leaders* (in connection with the Church) appears only five times and *leadership* only once. The term *pastors* just once. (Neither *leader* nor *pastor*, singular, shows up at all.) Paul and Peter each use a related plural word, *shepherds*, in both cases referring to elders. (*Shepherd*, singular, always appears in contexts pointing to Jesus.) But too often in a typically structured church gathering, the pastor does nearly everything: welcoming, preaching, praying, making announcements, offering the benediction, baptizing, and officiating at the Communion table. A pastor has the most access to and time with the microphone. Accepted church architecture puts the stage and pulpit—and thus the preacher—front and center.

The Silencing of the Laity

The loss of biblical balance in the matter of leadership began early in the history of the Church. In his discussion of the Greek word, *laikos* (which means belonging to the people, and from which our word *laity* comes), R. Paul Stevens says, "It is not used at all in the New Testament. Clement of Rome at the end of the first century was the first to use it for Christians. He used 'layman' (laikos) in his letter to the Corinthians to describe the place of laity in worship when the presbyters were being deprived of their functions."[34]

The muzzling of the so-called laity grew even more pronounced as time passed. Alan and Eleanor Kreider, in *Worship and Mission after Christendom*, quote from a church order in the *Apostolic Constitutions* (late fourth century), which "likened the church to a ship, in which the clergy were the 'mariners' and the people were 'passengers,' and it assigned to the deacons the tasks to 'watch the multitude and keep them silent.'"[35]

This out-of-biblical-balance emphasis on pastoral leadership continues today, negatively affecting both pastor and congregation. Most of us have seen statistics on pastoral burnout, marriage failures, and health issues. Writing for ChristianityToday.com, C. Christopher Smith says, "The language of 'going to church' (versus 'being the church' or 'belonging to a church') inclines us to think of church as a religious community where the clergy are professionals who do the work and churchgoers are basically consumers of religious goods and services. It's not difficult to see how this consumerist notion of church feeds into codependency and burnout."[36]

---

[34] Stevens, The Other Six Days, 27.

[35] Alan and Eleanor Kreider, *Worship and Mission after Christendom* (Harrisonburg, VA: Herald Press, 2011), 116.

[36] C. Christopher Smith, "The Koinonia Way," *Leadership Journal*, August 5, 2014, accessed April 15, 2016, http://www.christianitytoday.com/le/2014/august-online-only/koinonia-way.html.

Expecting too much of a single leader and too little of other members of the body underscores the wisdom of the plural leadership in New Testament churches.

But the traditional system shortchanges everyone else as well. I once spoke with an elder of a church whose pastor had left for a few months to serve as a military chaplain. The elder said: "We're just waiting for the pastor to get back so we can move ahead." In another church, a team of three was preparing to leave on a short-term mission trip to South America. The pastor called them to the front. Instead of letting them tell, in their own voices, the story of what they would be doing on their mission, he described their project himself. Instead of asking members of their small group to pray for them, he did so. Under such leadership, the people—as in the days when children were to be seen and not heard—are left with the impression they have nothing worthwhile to say.

One Sunday morning another pastor related how, during a leaders' meeting the previous week, he had asked how those in the group had seen God at work in their daily lives. He told the congregation that several in that session had responded with significant examples. However, rather than asking those same people to tell in their own voices what they had observed, he introduced his sermon by summarizing their answers in his own words. As happens far too often, efficiency and professionalism once again trumped one-anothering.

Commenting on a book recommending a management philosophy based on shared decision-making , one pastor wrote that he was aware he ought to be "much more decisive and direct" than that in his leadership approach. In a church setting, he said, the top leader "gets the vision from the Lord." He or she then passes the vision along to other church leaders and they carry it out. In the Old Testament, Moses got the vision from God. But where in the New Testament do we find any example of a single leader being solely responsible for obtaining the entire vision for a local church?

Perhaps this is why the late John Stott, at a convention in the year 2000, said: "Beware the papacy of the pastor." Unfortunately, many believe, he said, "not in the priesthood of all believers, but in the papacy of all pastors."[37]

In a website article, Karl Vaters has written:

The primary task of pastors is not to do the work of ministry. It's not to get people to buy into our vision. And it's certainly not to create a culture of dependency on us and our leadership skills. Our calling is to equip the saints. A church filled with people equipped to do the work of ministry is a well-led church. It's also a church that is more dependent on Jesus than on the pastor. Servant leadership is not about doing ministry for others. It's also not about getting them to do ministry for us. It's about helping other Jesus-followers be better Jesus-followers by being better Jesus-followers ourselves.[38]

Spending decades in a church where the professionals do all or most of the significant ministry can have effects comparable

---

[37] Lausanne Committee for World Evangelization, quoted in "Marketplace Ministry, Occasional Paper No. 40," (accessed July 9, 2010), https://www.lausanne.org/docs/2004forum/LOP40_IG11.pdf.

[38] Karl Vaters, New Small Church, "5 Cautions About Emphasizing Leadership over Followership," *New Small Church,* February 16, 2015, accessed April 15, 2016, http://newsmallchurch.com/leadership-over-followership/.

to long-term reliance on government handouts. Churches, like public agencies and businesses, can cultivate dependencies. In *Stewardship: Choosing Service over Self-Interest*, Peter Block urges leaders in companies and other organizations to embrace partnership instead of patriarchy. "In an organization, where those around us are all adults, taking responsibility for others' performance, learning, and future is a caretaking role that undermines of the most effective distribution of ownership and responsibility. This is why partnership is so critical to stewardship. It balances responsibility and is a clear alternative to parenting."[39]

A Water Shortage

Overstressing the roles of leaders results in underemphasizing what members of Christ's body should bring to the meeting of the congregation. When we assemble, we do so in our earthly bodies, which Paul compares to jars made of clay (2 Cor. 4:7). Our jars, he says, contain the treasure of Christ's light. Our jars also contain living water, because each one exercising faith in Jesus receives an artesian well, the life-giving Holy Spirit. As individuals, our jars hold a limited amount of living water. Coming together as believers should make available a fullness of that water not possible when we are alone. If our meeting formats permit only one or a few professionals to pour from their jars, we do receive a measure of living water. That stream does benefit the body of Christ. But we do not experience the *fullness* possible

---

[39] Peter Block, *Stewardship: Choosing Service over Self-Interest* (San Francisco: Berrett-Koehler Publishers, Inc., 1993), 27.

when the water flows from other jars God has filled with something to share. Just as a crimped garden hose checks the flow of water, traditions in which only one or two leaders are heard from restrict the stream of living water. We settle for puddles when God intends for us to drink from rivers.

Church Traditions: A Structure Too Small

A TV commercial for a pain reliever shows a man with flu symptoms moving about in a grossly undersized home. He reaches for a nasal tissue the size of a sticky note. Only by bending low can he manage to squeeze through the playhouselike doorway. His toothpick-sized thermometer almost disappears in his mouth. Calling the doctor is done on a phone that looks like it belongs in a dollhouse. He avoids banging his head on the ceiling by hunching over. That large man in those constricted quarters could serve as a parable for the body of Christ trying to function within the confines of the meeting format we call church.

Like the situation in the flu relief commercial, the tradition-shaped "house" of our meetings is too small for the "body" that is the Church. If we are to equip God's people to do their work of ministry—in both the gathered and scattered mode—we need to make certain that the shape of our church meetings actually moves us toward and not away from that goal.

In any church meeting, it is not only the one presenting the sermon who preaches. Just as the silent Creation speaks and proclaims (Ps. 19:1-4), all our traditions preach as well. Always naming worship rather than encouragement and mutual upbuilding as our purpose for gathering *preaches*. Meeting places built like theaters *preach*. Rank and file seating arrangements *preach*. Every element in the liturgy *preaches*. If one person almost always gives the sermon or if a team of teachers rotate, that choice also *preaches*. The question is: Are the messages preached by our traditions producing spectatoritis or one-anothering disciples?

CHAPTER 3

Making Disciples in Church as We Know It

> Disciplemaking must begin with a robust, biblically-based understanding and language for what it means to be conformed into the image of Christ for the sake of others. We must come to think, act and be like Jesus. The implementation of this portrait must have the power of the indwelling Spirit as the key catalyst for growth. Here we are not called to "try harder" but to "yield harder" to the will and word of God. The journey must be corporately and personally intentional. Haphazard pursuits will continue to yield flat results. All of this must be encased in authentic biblical community that begins with the nuclear family. For the community to be authentic it must allow participants to not only celebrate success but to confess struggle and unbelief without ostracism. Progressively becoming more like Christ is not a proverbial carrot that followers can never catch but a reality for us if we allow God to have his way in our lives.
>
> *Randy Frazee, Senior Minister,*
> *Oak Hills Church, San Antonio, TX,*
> *Author of Think, Act, Be like Jesus*

On a recent Sunday something unusual happened in our main congregational meeting: A young man ready to enter his first year at a university was given about five minutes to tell his story. He came from a home in which both parents were drug addicts. But he found his way to our church and became part of the youth group, which helped to strengthen him in his walk with Christ. On a short-term mission trip, he came to know the pastor who encouraged him to pursue a college degree. "I'll be the first in my family ever to go beyond high school," he told us. Spontaneous applause broke out when he finished speaking, and the entire congregation stood to their feet.

My wife and I simultaneously felt joy tempered with disappointment. Afterward we heard comments that reflected our own thinking: "That was wonderful! But we didn't even know him before this. And now he'll be leaving us and going off to school in another city." He had known the young people in the small youth group, the youth leaders, and the pastor, but was largely unknown in the congregation at large. Because he plans to major in business, I spoke with him afterward and promised to give him a book on serving Christ in the work world. Later I heard that another couple plans to send him money on a regular basis. Others probably responded in various ways as well. What made this experience during a Sunday gathering so unusual? A young man spoke. People responded. Members of the body of Christ were spurred into action. We had moved beyond spectatoritis.

This young man was in that age range now described as Millennials. Also known as Gen Y, such young people are increasingly asking for something more than spectatoritis. In his blog, *Holy Soup*, Thom Shultz says, "People are leaving their churches because they feel excluded. Excluded from participating in the communication of the message."[1]

---

[1] Thom S. Schultz, Holy Soup, "Done with 'Sit Down and Shut Up,'" *Holy Soup with Tom Schultz* (blog), June 9, 2015, accessed April 16, 2016,

Curing Sunday Spectatoritis

My concern is fueled not only by those who are leaving our churches but also by those who are staying. In the midst of a rapidly decaying culture, is the way we have come to "do church" equipping believers to permeate their spheres of influence with salt? Is what happens in a typical church gathering pulling its weight in the mission to produce disciples who shine the light of Christ into their workplaces, neighborhoods, and families? Or do our meeting formats reward those who are willing to sit, watch, and listen as others perform?

Alike Yet Different

Since that day when Jesus launched her to make disciples, the Church has plowed a long way through countless rough seas. The distance between any contemporary local church and the first-century church in, say, Ephesus, is staggering. Chronologically, we're more than 700,000 days apart. Geographically (at least for U.S. congregations), some five or six thousand miles separate us. Culturally, the gap stretches from camels to cell phones.

In spite of these great divides, what treasures do we and those first-century churches share in common? The same heavenly Father. The same Savior. The same Holy Spirit. The same promises of God. The same Gospel. The same assignments from Jesus. The same apostolic teachings (although no first century church had the complete New Testament). These are just a few examples of the spiritual treasures they knew and we still enjoy.

---

http://holysoup.com/2015/06/09/done-with-sit-down-and-shut-up/http://holysoup.com/2015/06/09/done-with-sit-down-and-shut-up/.

But we also have something they did not have—two millennia of church traditions, some of which we covered in the previous chapter. Still other traditions have taught all of us to think in a vocabulary completely foreign to those early believers. As a result, what those early believers took part in when they gathered was far from what we experience today as church. Consider these words so familiar to all of us today:

Denomination

Back then, they knew nothing of denominations, although Paul did warn in 1 Corinthians 1:12 against giving names to—denominating—various groups within the Church (as in the "Paulists," the "Apollonarians," the "Cephasites," and so on). Today, the Center for the Study of Global Christianity at Gordon-Conwell Theological Seminary estimates that in mid-2015 the world had 45,000 denominations.[2]

Clergy/Laity

Although the early church had leaders, the Gospels and New Testament letters make no distinction between *clergypersons* and *laypersons*. Yet today those terms have become so entrenched that we in the church not only think that way but have even taught the world that language as well.

Sacred/Secular

---

[2] "Christianity 2015: Religious Diversity and Personal Contact," *Gordon-Conwell Theological Seminary, International Bulletin of Missionary Research*39, no. 1 (January 2015), accessed April 19, 2016, http://www.gordonconwell.edu/ockenga/research/documents/1IBMR2015.pdf.

Although it knew the difference between the kingdoms of darkness and light, the first-century church perceived no gap between sacred and secular. The term *full-time Christian service* had not yet entered the lexicon of Christendom. The call to follow Christ was understood as a summons to serve him full time. The alternatives—half-time, spare-time, or no-time service—were not options. Yet today, young believers are challenged to step up to a "higher calling" with appeals like this (actual) one: "What about you? Is God calling you to full-time Christian service?"

Sermon

Look through most New Testament translations and you will search in vain for the word *sermon* (with the exception of some paraphrased versions). What we call Jesus's "Sermon on the Mount" is not so named in the Bible and only came to be called that hundreds of years later. Does Peter's message in Acts 2 correspond to today's weekly sermon? Hardly. He was speaking not to a congregation of believers but to non-Christians, calling them to repentance and faith. And he spoke dialogically. People could ask a question and hear him answer it.

Church Program

Those early Christians had never heard of a church program in the sense we use the word They had no VBS, no building programs, no aerobics classes, no baseball teams, no Easter-egg hunts. (One church even listed a meat-smoking program. Their group was called the Holy Smokers.) The ministries of those first-century believers were largely carried out in their households, their neighborhoods, their marketplaces, and their businesses. Now, of course, even modest-sized churches often have dozens of programs. These are not all bad but can easily suck people dry of the time needed for building real relationships in their life roles outside the organized church.

Church Service

When those first century Bible writers used the word *service*, they simply meant the act of serving God or helping others. Thanks to our traditions, though, we have given the word a new twist. To us it also means a church meeting.

Church Building

Christians in Rome, Ephesus, Corinth, and other cities gathered in homes. Church buildings were unknown until the third and fourth centuries. Meeting in homes kept the size of gatherings small. In *Paul's Idea of Community*, Robert Banks says, "the average membership was around thirty to thirty-five people."[3] Most believers today meet in church buildings. Today, according to Michael Bell, "half the churches in the United States have less than 75 people."[4] That is the situation with the size of churches. But when it comes to numbers of people, "half of church attenders in the U.S. go to churches larger than 400."[5]

Sanctuary

Hebrews 9:1 reminds us that those living under the Old Covenant had an "earthly sanctuary." Reflecting this, the Old Testament (NIV version) uses the word *sanctuary* more than 170

---

[3] Banks, *Paul's Idea of Community*, 35.
[4] Michael Bell, "What is an 'Average Church'?," *Internet Monk* (blog), July 13, 2009, accessed April 16, 2016, http://www.internetmonk.com/archive/michael-bell-what-is-an-average-church.
[5] Ibid.

times. In the New Testament, that word suddenly disappears as a reference to a set-apart place for Christians to gather and worship. Yet Christians today typically speak of the main room in a church building as a sanctuary. This word, too, has taken on new meaning in our day. We have animal sanctuaries, plant sanctuaries, and sanctuary cities. So the word now carries the connotation of escape from threatening circumstances and withdrawal to some protected place.

Church

Those first century Christians spoke of themselves as assemblies or gatherings (Greek, *ekklesia*). To them, the word simply meant all the believers in a province, city, or those who met in a house. Or it meant all believers in all places and all times from Pentecost on. By contrast, our English word *church* traces back not to *ekklesia* but to another Greek word, *kuriou*, meaning *Lord's* or *of the Lord*. Our word for church came to us through an Anglo Saxon word referring to the *Lord's house* or *house of the Lord*. And that house came to mean the building or meeting place.

This list of new and differently defined words could go on. The takeaway here is not that everything in the list is necessarily bad or sinful in itself. Instead, my point is that these terms and the practices they stand for make it clear that what we think of as church differs greatly from what those first Christians experienced when they gathered. We may be tempted to defend these customary church practices as biblical, when, in fact, they are traditional.

What Going to Church Now Means to Nearly Everyone

Suppose you were to invite several American Christians to dinner—all of them adults. Each regularly takes part with other believers in three kinds of gatherings: (a) a small group that meets midweek in a home, (b) a Sunday school class, and (c) a congregation that meets in a church building on the weekend. After the meal and over coffee and dessert, you ask your dinner guests which of these three is church. Based on what you know about how Christ-followers think and speak, what kinds of responses would you expect? No surprise when I conducted such an informal survey among those from institutional churches. All the respondents chose (c), the large group meeting in a church building.

Have you ever heard believers say they are going to church when they are on their way to meet with eight to twelve others in a home on a Wednesday evening? Likely not. To us, *Sunday school* means a class that meets on Sunday. It is never confused with the main weekly event. *Church* is that (usually) weekend gathering in a church building with the larger congregation.

Small groups and Sunday school classes are, in the minds of many, nice but optional. In many places, they are suspended for the summer months. Writing on *SmallGroups.com* (a ministry of *Leadership Journal*), Steve Cordle reports, "The stark reality is that more of America's church members stay away from home groups than attend them. Joseph Meyers writes that in the vast majority of churches, no more than 35 percent of the congregation participates in a home-based small group."[6]

If true, that leaves 65 percent or more whose church participation consists of the main congregational meeting. Going to church in the sanctuary of the church building is seen as the kind of gathering that matters most to God. Because *church* carries that kind of meaning within our Christian community, what we do in that congregational venue becomes critically important. Accordingly, we ought to make certain that what happens in those 60, 75, or 90 minutes is actually equipping believers to be fruitful disciples.

The Elephant Won't Go Away

The late Dallas Willard wrote: "Nondiscipleship is the elephant in the church. . . . The fundamental negative reality among Christian believers now is their failure to be constantly learning how to live their lives in The Kingdom Among Us."[7]

Estimates suggest the U.S. has more than 300,000 Protestant, Catholic, and Orthodox congregations.[8] Regardless of where, how, or when they meet, most churches include some sort of preaching or teaching, singing, prayer, and get-togethers within

---

[6] Steve Cordle, "Why Don't More People Attend Small Groups?," *SmallGroups.com,* June 12, 2006, accessed April 16, 2016, http://www.smallgroups.com/articles/2006/why-dont-more-people-attend-small-groups.html?paging=off.

[7] Dallas Willard, *The Divine Conspiracy: Rediscovering Our Hidden Life in God* (New York: HarperCollins Publishers, 1998), 301.

[8] U.S. Religion Census 2010: Summary Findings, accessed April 16, 2016, http://www.rcms2010.org/press_release/ACP%2020120501.pdf.

the weekly agenda. Clearly, excellent things are occurring in and through a great many of these congregations. Individuals carrying heavy loads of guilt are finding forgiveness of their sins. Formerly hopeless people are finding in Christ the courage to face the future unafraid. Outreach efforts are benefiting many in need. Through small groups of various kinds, constructive camaraderie is taking place. Thousands of congregations are hearing biblical teaching.

With all that going on every week, why does nondiscipleship hang on so persistently? In pointing out the prevalence of nondiscipleship, Willard is not alone. Many serious Christians are seeing and saying the same things.

I've found concerns about the lack of discipleship being expressed by church leaders of a variety of stripes. For example, David Platt, president of the Southern Baptist International Mission Board, has said, "the cost of non-discipleship is great for scores of people in the church sitting comfortably right now under the banner of Christianity, but have never counted the cost of following Christ—many eternally deceived."[9]

Tim McKnight, in the *MinistryU Blog* of the College of Christian Studies, Anderson University, describes "5 Reasons We Don't Make Disciples."[10] In a website article, "The Discipleship Crises," Michael Wallenmeyer writes about "Six Reasons We Don't

---

[9] David Platt, "The Tragic Cost of Non-Discipleship" (lecture), accessed April 16, 2016, http://worship.com/2013/07/the-tragic-cost-of-non-discipleship-david-platt/.

[10] Tim McKnight, "5 Reasons We Don't Make Disciples," *The MinistryU Blog* (blog), November 6, 2014, accessed April 16, 2016, http://auministry.com/5-reasons-disciples/.

Make Disciples."[11] Writing in *Charisma Magazine*, J. Lee Grady covers "7 Reasons We Don't Make Disciples."[12] Whether the reasons are five, six, or seven, the consensus confirms Dallas Willard's elephant-in-the-room analogy.

What explains this state of affairs? After decades of observing from both pew and pulpit—I will add another reason: at least one major contributor to nondiscipleship lies in the way so many church meetings amount to apprenticeships in passivity.

Spectatoritis helps explain why more than half of Millennials raised in church are leaving it behind, why only two out of ten in this age range consider involvement in church as important. These statistics alarm those concerned with what the church will be like in the decades to come. According to the Barna Group, "the first factor that will engage Millennials at church is as simple as it is integral: relationships."[13] Barna says, 36 percent of the Millennials surveyed said part of their problem with the church is the inability "to ask my most pressing life questions in church."[14]

---

[11] Michael Wallenmeyer, "Tag Archives: Reasons We Don't Make Disciples," *Michaelwallenmeyer.com* (blog), December 11, 2012, accessed April 16, 2016), http://michaelwallenmeyer.com/tag/reasons-we-dont-make-disciples/.

[12] J. Lee Grady, "7 Reasons We Don't Make Disciples," *Charisma Magazine,* April 2, 2014, accessed April 16, 2016, http://www.charismamag.com/blogs/fire-in-my-bones/20101-7-reasons-we-don-t-make-disciples.

[13] "5 Reasons Millennial Stay Connected to Church: Research Releases in Millennials & Generations," Barna Group, accessed April 16, 2016, https://www.barna.org/barna-update/millennials/635-5-reasons-millennials-stay-connected-to-church.html#.VudCWuaulSB.

[14] "Six Reasons Young Christians Leave Church: Research Releases in Millennials & Generations," Barna Group, accessed April 16, 2016,

Is it possible these young people are experiencing something akin to homesickness in their quest for relationships? Although most could undoubtedly not articulate it, are they pining for something that characterizes the core of what the New Testament teaches about church practice? And could it be that the relationships of costly, self-giving love provide the best clue as to why the first century church grew at such an astounding pace?

Yes, the New Testament churches experienced serious issues. Believers in the Jerusalem church failed to care for their Greek-speaking widows. Paul had to reprimand the church in Corinth for abuses in the way they ate the Lord's Supper. Euodia and Syntyche were at odds with each other in Philippi. All of these came from a breakdown in practicing the kind of one-anothering Jesus had called for in his new command. Yet in each case, when Paul wrote to correct these failures, he addressed his letter to the entire church. Everyone heard the letter when it was read. The deficiency in one-anothering was to be dealt with not by a handful of leaders but by the entire church. In other words, right one-anothering by the whole church was the antidote Paul prescribed to cure wrong one-anothering.

Today our inherited church traditions will not provide relief from the disease of spectatoritis. The "way we've always done it" only prolongs the illness. Restricting participation in our congregational meetings can give an appearance of unity and conceal the kinds of issues that surfaced in New Testament

---

https://www.barna.org/barna-update/millennials/528-six-reasons-young-christians-leave-church#.VuG76TY-9YO.

churches. But curbing one-anothering in those gatherings simply keeps such problems out of sight—temporarily.

Obeying Jesus's new command to practice one-anothering and extending it into our main-church meeting formats will expose our failures and provide the body of Christ with the multimembered resources it needs to deal with them. One-anothering should serve as a primary molding influence as we decide how we ought to meet together in the twenty-first century. As noted in the beginning of Chapter One, Elton Trueblood told us how to cure Sunday Spectatoritis: "The secret is participation, participation, participation."

Making the Best Use of Our Time Together

Soon after our children were born, I had one of those aha moments. The insight struck hard: We would have just a few short years with these developing people. Assuming their leaving home at 18 and living to be 90, the in-home time with us would total only 20 percent of their lives. In reality, of course, the percentage would be far lower after subtracting in-school time, with-friends time, and the like. The takeaway was inescapable: If we were to help these young ones mature into responsible, God-loving adults, we needed to make the best use of the limited time they would spend with us. The way we would shape the activities in our home at the "launch pad" would exert a powerful molding effect on the other 80-plus percent of our children's lives.

When it comes to the time Christ-followers spend together as the gathered church, the percentages are many times smaller. For those who participate only in a once-per-week meeting of, say,

90 minutes, the yearly gathered time is not even 80 hours. That is less than one percent of their annual allotment of about 8700 hours. For others, who may spend another two hours a week with fellow believers in a small group plus 90 minutes in a congregational setting, the 182 hours of gathered time adds up to barely more than two percent. Pie charts dramatize the miniscule amounts of time in the first and second case:

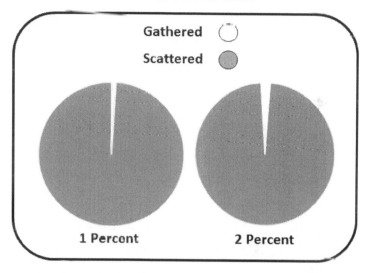

Again, the point is obvious: If we are aiming to make disciples, as Jesus calls us to do, we must make the best possible use of the tiny fund of gathered time available in what Christians perceive as church. But what is the best possible use? How can we shape that precious gathered time into an instrument that will actually cultivate disciples who love and serve Jesus and others?

On an encouraging note, some of our cherished church traditions can actually be transformed and harnessed to pull their weight in one-anothering. As will be seen in the accounts from churches presented in Chapter Six, some pastors and church leaders have learned creative ways to do just that. Here are some examples:

Sermons.

Years of conditioning lead us to think of sermons as being synonymous with lectures—spoken presentations before groups of people to inform them about some topic. We typically think of sermons in terms of monologues—one person presenting an uninterrupted address. Nowhere, though, does Scripture require teaching or preaching to take that form. Two of the churches in Chapter Six have successfully transitioned to dialogical (think *dialogue*) sermons.

Alan and Eleanor Kreider, in *Worship and Mission after Christendom*, call for bringing the voices of the congregation back into sermons. "Opportunities to respond, or report back, could be constructive, for they indicate ways in which God's proclaimed word interacts with the congregation as it participates in God's mission. If this is to happen . . . pastors may need to recast their sermons. . . . And they may need to make their sermons more dialogical."[15]

In his article, "Interactive Preaching," Stuart Murray Williams discusses how an alternative to monological preaching might look:

> This might mean drawing the congregation into sermons by asking questions, inviting responses, welcoming insights. It might mean discussion groups during or after sermons. It might mean changing the way the chairs are arranged to make dialogue

---

[15] Kreider, *Worship and Mission after Christendom*, 122.

and discussion possible. It might mean having two speakers debating an issue together, with congregational participation. It might mean asking several people to reflect on a passage for a week and then construct a sermon together. It might mean inviting a congregation to do some preparatory reading during the week so that they can contribute thoughtfully to a teaching period. It might mean developing a culture where people know they are free to interrupt and interject comments.[16]

In the first century, Jesus used a highly dialogical method for teaching his disciples. And in our century, this still seems to be the preferred way of communicating. We now have talk radio, where hosts invite callers to interact with them on important issues. I have heard seminary graduates say the most meaningful courses were those in which—at least part of the time—the professor engaged class members in a back-and-forth conversation.

Baptisms

Just as the New Testament does not prescribe monological sermons, neither does it offer us any rule that gives only pastors the right to baptize. Apparently Jesus (John 4:2) and presumably Paul (1 Cor. 1:15-17) delegated the work of baptizing to those they were training. In at least three of the churches whose practices are described in Chapter Six, baptisms are performed by a variety of believers. Even a Baptist pastor transitioned to this way of putting

---

[16] Stuart Murray Williams, "Interactive Preaching," *The Anabaptist Network,* March 3, 2008, accessed January 30, 2016, http://www.anabaptistnetwork.com/node/322.

one-anothering ministry into the hands of nonpastors! Many churches schedule baptisms as part of their main gathering. This, then, presents another excellent opportunity for participation in the context of the whole congregation.

Communion

In one church example in Chapter Six, young people (Millennials) from the ages of 17 to 24 are invited to pray over the bread and cup before the elements are distributed to the congregation. A pastor from that congregation told me the congregation sometimes files down to the front to receive the elements. On those Sundays people who may not have a public role hold the elements. Chapter Six also describes how one church made Communion a part of a congregational meal.

Prayer

This does not have to be limited to what has become widely known as the pastoral prayer in the weekly gathering of a congregation. Three of the churches in Chapter Six have discovered ways of involving members of the body to pray for one another without putting anyone on the spot. Although it has been more than ten years since one man participated in a church that practiced this one-anothering kind of prayer on Sunday morning, he recalls how powerful and transformative it was in his life and, he is confident, in the lives of others who still believe in praying for one another, as the Scripture exhorts.

Testimonies

Although they fell widely out of use some years ago, testimonies remain a powerful tool in disciple-making. The Kreiders explain why they are seldom heard these days:

"Testimony is a term that bores some people and alarms others. It bores people because at times testimonies are oft-repeated stories about long-ago conversion experiences. . . . Testimony in worship alarms people when the stories become embarrassingly personal."[17] To avoid these connotations, some suggest calling testimonies "reports from the front lines." Others call them "FaithStories." But whatever we call these spoken accounts, the Kreiders emphasize their importance in our gatherings:

> If we receive no reports from the front in our congregations, we are in trouble. Without testimonies we experience a drought, a nutritional deficit for healthy Christian living. And the dominant cultural narratives take over. God seems powerless and inactive. And Christians who do see evidence of the missional activities of God in our time may only whisper about it in the church's hallways or discuss it during the week in house groups or on the telephone—but not in worship services.[18]

During the episode "As You Were" in the television series, *White Collar*, FBI Agent Clinton Jones tells Neal Caffrey that sacrifice "means giving up something that you want for something that you want more."[19] Which do we want more, church traditions or real one-anothering? Are we willing to sacrifice the one for the other? We need to fashion our gatherings in ways that permit the many-membered church to reach maturity. Paul, the "expert builder" (1 Cor. 3:10), followed that path in his own church-

---

[17] Kreider, *Worship and Mission after Christendom*, 82.
[18] Ibid., 83.
[19] White Collar, "As You Were," episode 8, July 26, 2011.

planting work. In his letters to churches, he used the Greek term *allelon* (translated as one another or each other) some 35 times in a church-related context—a clear indication that he saw one-anothering as central to church life.

But the rationale for one-anothering goes much deeper than just the New Testament usage of *allelon*. As we shall see in the next chapter, the case for one-anothering also rests on the makeup of the Church as the body of Christ.

CHAPTER 4

The Case for One-Anothering as We Gather

Every day the veracity of God's love is revealed through
Christ's body, the Church. Nowhere is the members' conveyance of
sincere faith and the application of their genuine gifts more needed
than in the urban centers of our world. The practice of one-anothering
among believers instinctively extends an embrace to the vulnerable,
hospitality to the stranger, and care for the orphans and widows
among us. One-anothering doesn't separate the church from the city
or community; it incarnates Christ as the lover of the world and his
children as loving participants in its restoration and redemption! This
chapter makes space for relationships between followers of Christ that
strengthen His mission to the entire world—including its burgeoning
global cities. Gathered, they "spur one another on to good works," and
scattered they touch every "spiritually darkened place" with the in-
breaking Kingdom of Light and Love.

Susan Spousta, Affinity Network Coordinator,
The Foursquare Church, Portland, OR

If our usual ways of following church traditions are not to
determine the shape of our church meetings, what should do so?
Before taking up that question, let's imagine a couple of ridiculous
scenes:

- You have just arrived at the gym for a workout. You step
  onto an elliptical machine, adjust the settings, and get set
  for 30 minutes of cardio. But once there, you notice that

only two parts of you are working. Your left hand takes a firm grip on one handle and your left arm pushes and pulls your hand to pump the lever. The rest of you does not budge. This happens not just once but over and over again for years. A decade later, your left arm is buff and full of stamina. But elsewhere what should be strong muscles have turned to flab.

- It is dinner time, so the seven members of your family head into the dining room. But the table has been removed. Instead, three rows of chairs—two in each row—face toward a single chair which is turned toward the six. You, your four siblings, and Mom sit in the rows, while Dad sits in the lone chair up front. The "conversation" consists almost entirely of Dad giving instructions on what to think and how to act. Anything Mom and the kids may say has been prewritten for them by someone else. After reaching the empty nest stage, your parents puzzle over why their adult children are so indecisive and unprepared to take on responsibility.

What makes each of these situations so ludicrous? In the first, all the members of a body need to exercise and to work together if each is to develop properly and become strong. In the second case, when it gathers for a meal, a family should sit in a way each can see all the others. And everyone, young or old, should have the opportunity to interact with others in the family— sharing experiences, offering advice, providing encouragement, or asking questions. The New Testament, of course, speaks of the Church as both a body and a family. In each, all the members need the freedom to carry out their intended purposes.

Growth Happens as Christ Reveals Himself through His Body

Through what medium do we reveal ourselves to others? Let us say you have just passed along a report to a friend who doubts its validity: she raises an eyebrow. You meet someone on the sidewalk who, despite repeated promises to pay, still owes you money: he diverts his eyes. If you are meeting someone for the first time, what does the handshake tell you if it is firm? Finger-crushing? Fishlike? You are interviewing someone your company may hire, but she is slouching in her chair. What is she revealing about herself? Even our walk says something about us. Do we strut? Slink? Shuffle? What makes us laugh or cry? In other words, we reveal ourselves to others through the members of our bodies.

In a typical Sunday church meeting, what part of Christ's body does the congregation have most opportunity to see and hear? The pastor. No matter how godly and devoted, the pastor— who plays a very prominent and important teaching/preaching role—is just one member in the body. Christ can reveal some of himself through the pastor's life and words. But he can reveal himself in fullness only as other members of his body act and speak as well.

You have probably heard this statement many times: A church reflects the disposition of its pastor. Absorbing the traits of the pastor may occur in just three years. Megachurch pastor T. D. Jakes says, "I know from years of being an evangelist that churches take on the personality of their pastors."[1] Jakes's observation is spot on. But should that be the case? Whose personality should a church be taking on? We are to have the "mind of Christ" (1 Cor. 2:16). Our "attitude should be the same as that of Christ Jesus" (Phil. 2:5). We are to "walk as Jesus did" (1 John 2:6).

How can Jesus fully reveal himself? The same way we reveal ourselves—through the members of his body. Just as others know us through our mouths, eyes, hands, and feet, we come to know the richness of Jesus as he expresses himself through the various members of his body.

Each Part a Working Part

When one of our granddaughters was not yet two years old, she stopped growing. Doctors said she had fallen off the charts. Diagnosis: her pituitary gland had stopped producing enough of her own growth hormone. One part of her was not working—and that affected all the other parts. Treatment: supplementing the output of the sluggish gland with shots, which continued for several years. Today, she is a normal-sized, healthy adult.

Spiritually, stunted growth afflicts a myriad of Christ-followers. Christian leaders generally agree that far too many

---

[1] Jessica Martinez, "TD Jakes Tells Church Leaders 'If You're Not Making any Change, You're Taking Up Space,'" *CP Church & Ministry,* March 10, 2014, accessed April 16, 2016, http://www.christianpost.com/news/td-jakes-tells-church-leaders-if-youre-not-making-any-change-youre-taking-up-space-115914/.

born-again Christians get stuck in the milk stage, failing to mature
and produce fruit.

- Greg Ogden called it a "discipleship deficit."[2]

- As noted in Chapter Three, Dallas Willard called it
  "nondiscipleship" and tagged it as the "elephant in the
  church."[3]

- A Barna Group report said, "our studies this year
  among pastors showed that almost nine out of ten
  senior pastors of Protestant churches asserted that
  spiritual immaturity is one of the most serious
  problems facing the Church."[4]

Countless treatment plans have been proposed to deal with
this growth deficiency. Many of them have had encouraging
results. Seldom if ever, though, have I heard anyone connect
nondiscipleship with the way Paul says the body of Christ moves
toward maturity. In Ephesians 4:16, one of the many places Paul
speaks of the Church as a body, he describes—with just a few
strokes of his pen—one of the most important insights into how
spiritual growth happens: "From him [Christ] the whole body,
joined and held together by every supporting ligament, grows and
builds itself up in love, as each part does its work."

---

[2] Greg Ogden, "The Discipleship Deficit: Where Have all the Disciples
Gone?," *Knowing & Doing* (Spring 2011), accessed April 16, 2016,
http://www.cslewisinstitute.org/The_Discipleship_Deficit_page1.

[3] Willard, *The Divine Conspiracy,* 301.

[4] "Barna Studies the Research, Offers a Year-in-Review Perspective,"
Barna Group, December 20, 2009, accessed April 16, 2016,
https://www.barna.org/barna-update/faith-spirituality/325-barna-studies-the-
research-offers-a-year-in-review-perspective#.VudfZOaulSB.

"From him . . . ." The growth process emanates from Christ himself. His life streams into "the whole body." The bonding of the body is achieved not by one or a handful of its members but by "every supporting ligament." The goal is realized as the body "grows and builds itself up in love." How? By what means or process does this growth occur? It happens "as each part does its work."

Paul does not say that the spiritual growth occurs as a few parts do the work. Nor does he say that the body of Christ grows as one part does the lion's share of the work. Instead, he emphasizes that the growth comes as each part shoulders its share of the task. God designed the body of Christ with multiple working parts. By implanting his Spirit in every part, he gave each believer the capacity to contribute to the growth of others. In allergy relief tablets the inactive ingredients may greatly outnumber the active ingredients. That apparently works in Claritin®, but not in the church, where God's design calls for all members of the body to be "active ingredients," even in church meetings. Anything less fosters spectatoritis.

David Peterson wonders why this kind of active involvement is missing in our main congregational gatherings:

> First Corinthians 14 surely speaks to us of the value and importance of spontaneous, verbal ministries of exhortation, comfort or admonition by the congregational members (cf. 1 Thess. 4:18; 5:11, 14; Eph. 4:15). Such mutual ministry is often confined to the home group, or to times of personal interaction

after church services. Why is it not also encouraged in the public gathering of the whole church?[5]

Each part's ability to do its work depends on Spirit-given gifts. Consider 1 Corinthians 12:7 in these four translations:

- "Now to each one the manifestation of the Spirit is given for the common good" (*NIV*).
- "A spiritual gift is given to each of us so we can help each other" (*NLT*).
- "The Holy Spirit displays God's power through each of us as a means of helping the entire church" (*The Living Bible*).
- "To each person the manifestation of the Spirit is given for the benefit of all" (*New English Translation*).

Paul does not leave this work to be done by each part as an optional assignment. What each part has received is for *the entire church* and for *the benefit of all*—not simply a small segment of it. Although Christ builds his Church (Matt. 16:18), he has given to every member of his body the dignity and responsibility of partnership in the building project. Building up is the point in each of these passages:

- "Each of us should please his neighbor [fellow believer] for his good, to build him up" (Rom. 15:2).
- ". . . try to excel in gifts that build up the church" (1 Cor. 14:12).

---

[5] David Peterson and I. Howard Marshall, *Engaging with God: A Biblical Theology of Worship* (Downers Grove, IL: InterVarsity Press, 1992), 197.

- ". . . therefore encourage one another and build each other up" (1 Thess. 5:11).

In choosing these building terms, Paul is using the same language as he employed in Eph. 4:16. Each part doing its work is what builds the body of Christ and causes it to grow. So in Paul's mind, each member of the body is a church builder. Because "each member belongs to all the others" (Rom. 12:5), it is important that those others be given opportunity to benefit from each member. That is possible only when the whole church body gathers. If this or that member of the body has opportunity to do its work only in a fraction, a subgroup, of the church, his or her giftedness is unavailable to all the others. This is especially true if most of those others never take part in a small group.

Creating a One-Anothering Environment

Paul leaves no doubt that every believer houses one or more God-given aptitudes that others in the body need for reaching spiritual maturity. It follows that church leaders ought to design meeting formats in which those gifts can find expression. In his book, *Joy at Work*, Dennis Bakke argues for a business leadership style that delegates decision-making to those doing the work. He says, "the role of leaders is to create an environment that allows these qualities [motivation, discipline, and inner strength] to flourish."[6] In the church context, we might paraphrase it this way: The role of church leaders is to create and maintain an

---

[6] Dennis W. Bakke, *Joy at Work: A Revolutionary Approach to Fun on the Job* (Seattle, WA: PVG, 2005), 135.

environment in which each member of the body of Christ may do his or her work.

My shoulder is currently reminding me of the importance of each member playing its intended part. The doctor, after examining X-rays, pronounced it to be calcific tendonitis. Whatever its name, the impairment in the shoulder limits what my right arm and hand can do—which in turn hampers my entire body. Each part must be able to contribute its work for the whole body to function as intended.

What happens if a church-meeting environment does not extend freedom for the various parts to function? Think straitjacket. Even if just the arm-parts of the body are encased and strapped, the body will not be able to carry out all the work it was designed to do. How much more disabled a body becomes if the ankles are shackled and the mouth is duct-taped shut. Even with all those restrictions, of course, the body remains alive and can function to some degree (breathing, twisting, listening, thinking, and so on). The point: If any part of the body cannot do its work, the entire body loses the benefits of what that part was designed to contribute.

In the Church some parts of the body are teacher-parts. James 3:1 warns that "not many" should become teachers. Notice this, though: James does not say that only one should be recognized as teacher. Yet if the meeting format almost always limits the teaching to just one voice, any others with that gift must sit in silence. If virtually all the teaching comes through just one member, the other members will miss fullness in what they hear. Even Paul, recipient of tremendous revelation from God's Spirit, said that he knew "in part" (1 Cor. 13:12). Let us say that in a certain congregation of 100 people, three percent have received the gift of teaching. That means that the richness of instruction from those recognized as gifted teachers should be coming through at least three members of the body.

Every part doing its proper work for the good of all the other parts—in an environment that permits that work to take place—amounts to mutual responsibility. That is another way of saying one-anothering. This is the principle that should guide us as we shape our regular get-togethers. And, as already covered in Chapter One, this lines up perfectly with what Jesus called his new command.

One-Anothering Takes Knowing Each Other

In *The Equipping Pastor,* R. Paul Stevens and Phil Collins relate what a long-term pastor told the congregation in his farewell sermon: "He was deeply loved by the people he had served for many years. No one would deny the integrity with which he cared for the people He was widely regarded as 'successful.' But as he reflected on the result of his pastoral ministry, he made a revealing comment: 'I know every one of you. And every one of you knows me. But you do not know each other!'"[7] I suspect the same could be said of most who attend churches in the U.S.

Not long ago I had a conversation with a woman in her 80s who had been part of her church for decades. A few days before

---

[7] R. Paul Stevens and Phil Collins, *The Equipping Pastor: A Systems Approach to Congregational Leadership* (Durham, NC: The Alban Institute, 1993), 19.

she had just heard for the first time another Christian woman about her age share some insights about her own walk of faith. They both were long-term members of the same church. "Why is it," the first woman asked me, "that we have to wait until someone's funeral to know any of their story?"

Not knowing each other makes it impossible to practice what Jesus called for in his new command—which he gave in its highly condensed form. Just as a prism separates white light into its beautiful array of colors, the New Testament letters refract the light of the new command into dozens of one-anothering instructions. Each of these defines a specific way of loving each other as Jesus has loved us. It names a particular means of laying down our lives for each other. Some of these one-anothering commands identify attitudes we are to maintain toward other believers—living in harmony, being kind, accepting, forgiving, and so on. Others describe concrete action steps, tangible one-anothering practices:

- Greeting
- Praying For
- Encouraging
- Spurring On
- Teaching/Instructing
- Serving
- Confessing

If a church meeting is structured in ways that permit believers to do these things regularly, over time they will get to know each other. When practiced with the New Testament one-anothering attitudes, these one-anothering actions during a congregational gathering can transform individuals as well as the corporate body. As it carries out these actions, the body of Christ "grows and builds itself up in love as each part does its work" (Eph. 4:16).

One-Anothering and the Kingdom of God

Of course we must never lose sight of the big picture as we practice one-anothering in our church meetings. More than 50 times, Jesus and the Gospel writers refer to the Kingdom of God. From the opening of his public ministry, Jesus spoke of the coming near of the Kingdom of God as the good news. He also taught us to pray that the Kingdom would come and that God's will be done on earth as in heaven. Seeking first God's Kingdom is the big picture.

Why is it so vital that each part do its work in a context of one-anothering? Because that is how we shore each other up with reports of what has been called the present in-breaking of God's Kingdom. As George Eldon Ladd puts it in *The Gospel of the Kingdom*, "the Kingdom of God has invaded this present evil Age that man may know something of its blessings even while the evil Age goes on."[8] In this evil Age where we receive so much bad news, we all need to hear how God's will is being done right here on earth in the context of our weekday lives—our neighborhoods, families, and workplaces. If the meeting environment provides opportunity for one-anothering, Christians will find openings to

---

[8] George Eldon Ladd, *The Gospel of the Kingdom* (Grand Rapids, MI: Wm. B. Eerdmans Publishing Company, 1959), 42.

act as good news reporters of what God is doing in their particular corners of his Kingdom.

A Kingdom-Related One-Anothering Strategy

Seen biblically, one-anothering is a vital part of the big picture, the Kingdom-of-God perspective. Any church can make one-anothering one of its key meeting strategies—not the only one, but a primary one. A strategy stands midway between mission and tactics, each of which must be clearly stated. Here, for example, is how a church might spell out its mission-strategy-tactics set:

Overall Kingdom Mission:

To serve, in word and deed, as the world's salt and light—those sent by Jesus into every one of its spiritually decaying and darkened places.

Meeting Strategy:

Through one-anothering as we gather,
to strengthen each other for our mission
by mutually building up fellow members of Christ's body.

Meeting Tactics:

Greeting One Another

Praying for One Another

Encouraging One Another

Spurring on One Another

Teaching/Instructing One Another

Serving One Another

Confessing Sins to One Another

Chapter Five elaborates on each of these one-anothering actions and its vital place in body life. Then Chapter Six illustrates

Curing Sunday Spectatoritis

these with 25 examples of how churches are shaping their main weekly gatherings to provide opportunities for one or more of the seven one-anothering actions.

CHAPTER 5

One-Anothering Actions

In *The Fire Next Time*, James Baldwin wrote: "There are too many things we do not wish to know about ourselves." One Anothering causes us to think introspectively about our proclivities as believers. Chapter Five presents the "How to" and it provokes the question, Are we willing to go beyond the demureness of accepted religious practice in order to grow in fellowship and love? The Baldwin quote speaks to inhibitions; by contrast, the pursuit of the seven One Anothering Actions beckons believers to reach beyond familiarity for the express purpose of knowing and respecting the work of God in one another. Urban life is complex and quite often urban congregations struggle to make fluid adaptations due to rigorous adherence to well-intended traditions. Weekly One Anothering in many African American congregations can be summed up in the tradition of "Call and Response" during the preaching event. I am convinced that the practice of One Anothering can enhance the Christian experience in any context.

Rodney DeWitt Robinson-Rogers, Senior Pastor,
Christ of Calvary Covenant Church, Philadelphia, PA,

When we get together, at least seven of the New Testament one-another commands involve outward actions that can become elements in our congregational meetings. Each of these actions becomes a specific way of loving one another as Jesus has loved us. Each involves the laying down of our lives for the benefit of other Christians. This chapter will explore how these seven one-anothers have an essential place in the growth and building up of the body of Christ.

Greeting One Another

How can church leaders shape church meetings in ways that incorporate meaningful greetings? The answer may not be as simple as we imagine. Many churches include a greeting time at or near the beginning of each congregational meeting. Typically the pastor or someone else instructs everyone to stand and extend a welcome to others. If you are there and hear this invitation, it means you have perhaps 60 seconds to reach left, right, and forward, and to pivot backward to shake hands. If the greeting involves an exchange of names, it can be difficult to hear above the voices of the crowd.

Some see the greeting time as the highlight of the meeting; others hardly endure it. Thom Rainier conducted an informal survey asking guests why they decided not to give a church a second visit. To his surprise, the top response was having to stand up and greet others. Among the comments: "I would rather have a root canal than be subjected to a stand and greet time."[1] When they hear "let's all stand and greet each other," most Christians probably fall somewhere on the enthusiasm-antipathy continuum.

In their letters, both Paul (2 Cor. 13:12) and Peter (1 Pet. 5:14) urge Christ-followers to practice this form of one-anothering.

---

[1] Comment on Thom S. Rainier, "Top Ten Ways Churches Drive Away First-Time Guests," *Thom S. Rainer* (blog), November 1, 2014, accessed April 16, 2016, http://thomrainer.com/2014/11/top-ten-ways-churches-drive-away-first-time-guests/.

The Greek word usually translated as *greet* (*aspazomai*) occurs nearly 60 times in the New Testament. It apparently came from a term meaning *to enfold in the arms*. The idea is to welcome, to embrace, to receive joyfully. When Paul and Peter wrote their reminders to greet one another, they probably did not imagine how these instructions would be followed in our time. Aside from most not practicing the holy kiss, at least two major differences stand out.

First, many churches place a great deal of emphasis on greeting first-time visitors in the hope that they will choose that congregation and settle in. While visitors should be greeted, the New Testament calls for greeting *one another*. In other words, this is one way of laying down our lives, sacrificing our own comfort or agenda, for established members of the body—not only visitors—to build each other up.

Second, many congregations delegate this ministry to greeters who stand at the door. Sometimes teams rotate this responsibility. This practice may be helpful. But in saying one another, Paul and Peter put this responsibility on *everyone*. They did not provide an escape clause that let Christians forget about greeting unless it happens to be their turn on an official greeting team.

A sincere and attentive greeting carries profound meanings:

- You are accepted (just as God accepts us).
- You are valuable (made in God's image, someone God treasures).
- You are safe (just as we are secure in Christ).

- You are loved (just as God loves us).

These meanings leave no doubt how vital it is for believers to be taught how to greet and to be given opportunities to do so in meaningful (and not merely ritualistic) ways. At least two of the reports from churches (Chapter Six) show that this is possible in contemporary congregations.

Praying For One Another

When James wrote, "Pray for each other" (5:16), he certainly meant we are to include other believers in our private prayers. But if the practice of the New Testament church James knew tells us anything, it also means praying when we meet together. Consider these examples:

- "They all joined together constantly in prayer" (Acts 1:14).
- "Then they prayed" (Acts 1:24).
- "They devoted themselves . . . to prayer" (Acts 2:42).
- ". . . they raised their voices together in prayer to God" (Acts 4:31).
- ". . . he [Peter] went to the house of Mary . . . where many people had gathered and were praying" (Acts 12:12).

Today, although some churches still practice corporate praying, in others it seems different priorities have pushed it to the sidelines. In many congregations, the only praying done in the main congregational meeting is offered by the pastor and perhaps by the people reciting the Lord's Prayer. Does this help explain why, when Christians assemble in small groups, so few are willing to pray out loud in front of others? Indeed, praying for one another in the presence of one another does involve laying down our lives for one another, moving us out of our individual comfort zones.

Jesus left no doubt that he considered the Jewish temple, God's house in those days, as a "house of prayer" (Matt. 21:13). But as he also made clear, that house was left "desolate" (Matt. 23:38), deserted, forsaken, uninhabited. Did that spell the end of the house of God as a house of prayer? Not at all. Today, the Church is the house of God (Heb. 3:6; 1 Pet. 2:5; 4:17). Now the *ecclesia* is God's house of prayer. Some of the churches described in Chapter Six include praying for one another in their main congregational gatherings.

Encouraging One Another

Encourage one another. Spur each other on. What is the difference? They undoubtedly overlap, but New Testament writers seem to make a distinction between them. Encouragement rekindles believing, while spurring on fires up doing. In Acts 14:22, Paul was "encouraging [believers] to remain true to the faith." In Hebrews 14:24, the writer of Hebrews urged Christ-followers to "spur one another on toward love and good deeds."

Encouragement is often needed when the faith-fire burns low and needs stoking. Jesus was encouraging his disciples when he told them, "Do not let your hearts be troubled. Trust in God; trust also in me" (John 14:1). Trusting involves faith, believing. Spurring on is called for when weary believers need prodding to get back to work. Jesus was spurring on believers in Ephesus when he urged them to "do the things you did at first" (Rev. 2:5). Doing involves deeds, work, action.

Encouraging one another can, does, and should happen in small groups but is not limited to that context. Four one another/each other passages in the New Testament speak of our responsibility for mutual encouragement (1 Thess. 4:18; 5:11; Heb. 3:13; 10:25). Most versions translate the Greek word *parakaleo* as *encourage*. Others render it as *comfort*, *exhort*, or *warn*. In the verses just referenced, encouragement seems to be an antidote against:

- The damaging effects of grief and loss.
- The erosion of faith, hope, and love.
- Growing hard as a result of being deceived by sin.
- Swerving from the faith and turning away from God.

How often does the typical Christian, facing hurt, doubt, and temptation in encounters throughout the week—school, neighborhood, work, home—need to hear encouragement from other members of the body? The author of Hebrews apparently saw a constant and recurring need for such rekindling (Heb. 3:13).

Spurring One Another On

Growing up on an asparagus farm explains my distaste for this green vegetable that most consider delicious. The harvesting season ran from late April until roughly the Fourth of July. Dad hired high school students as his cutting crew. The work began at 5 a.m. and lasted until time to leave for school. Each teenager had to bend over to plunge what looked something like a long-handled putty knife below the ground, slicing loose what we nicknamed the "grass" one spear at a time.

Plenty of factors conspired to turn the kids into laggards. Dad, however, had developed a carefully thought-out strategy to keep the crew on task. Whenever he noticed someone falling behind the rest of the pack, he would simply join the dawdler and begin cutting alongside him or her. Most of the time, he did not have to say a word. Years afterward students gratefully remembered having learned good work habits from George Peabody.

Like that asparagus crew, we Christians can become foot-draggers when it comes to living out the love and good works God has called us to. That was apparently as much the case in the first century as it is today. Which explains why Paul instructed the Thessalonian brothers and sisters—the whole church, not just their leaders—to "warn those who are idle" (1 Thess. 5:14). And which also explains why the writer of Hebrews called for the kind of one-anothering that would fire them up again: "And let us consider how we may spur one another on toward love and good deeds" (Heb. 10:24). Might these writers have been thinking of Jesus's call to let our light shine through our good works (Matt. 5:16)? Unless we mutually keep on stirring such actions back to life, weariness, discouragement, and lack of visible results will cause them to atrophy.

The Greek word for *spur on* carries the idea of intense yet well-meant incitement to action. *Consider* tells us this kind of re-motivating stimulation should not be done lightly or off the top of one's head. It means to be concerned enough about these spurrings-on to give them careful reflection and attention.

Curing Sunday Spectatoritis

Having served as a pastor, I know that some of the most effective spurring on comes from one's peers in the trenches. Suppose a believer who works all week as an accountant for the government has nearly given up on shining the light of Christ because of all the emphasis on separation of church and state. Imagine the impact of hearing another government employee tell how God has shown her effective ways to live out her faith in a public agency without running afoul of the law.

If it is true that 65 percent of church people do not take part in small groups, where will they receive any regular spurring on by other believers? Is it possible that discipleship today so often lacks horsepower because so few church meeting formats provide a place for spurs?

Teaching/Instructing One Another

On Sundays, most Protestant churches make the sermon central, giving it the most time and prominence in the church meeting. While the delivery of a sermon is generally called preaching, the bulk of its content should—in most cases—more accurately be called teaching. To some degree the two activities overlap in the New Testament. Generally, though, preaching (from Greek words like *kerysso, angello,* and *evangelizomai*) has to do with heralding or announcing the good news of salvation through faith in Christ. Teaching (from terms like *katecheo* and *didasko*) is instruction given to those who have already believed the good news, helping them understand how to live it out in every sphere of life.

What do the New Testament letters teach about teaching? There is no simple answer to that question. Paul, John, and the author of Hebrews present us with several truths about teaching, some of which seem paradoxical. For example, consider summaries of these passages:

- God has appointed teachers in and for the church (1 Cor. 12:28; Eph. 4:11).
- Not many should be teachers (Jas. 3:1).
- All believers should be able to teach and instruct each other (Rom. 15:14; Col. 3:16).
- Teaching is a gift given by the Holy Spirit (Rom. 12:7).
- Elders should be able to teach (1 Tim. 3:2; Tit. 1:9).
- Immature believers need someone to teach them beginners' truth (Heb. 5:12).
- Maturity, generally speaking, ought to make Christians into teachers (Heb. 5:12).
- The anointing of God's Spirit means Christians do not need anyone to teach them (1 John 2:27).

What are we to make of these statements that seem to be saying such different things? When it comes to teaching, what does the Church need? (a) None at all? (b) Teaching by its official teachers alone? (c) Instruction from fellow believers? Or (d) Teaching both by official teachers and fellow believers? Harmonizing these passages on teaching, I believe, leads us to (d).

In our contemporary setting, most Christians look to those officially recognized as having authority to teach—a pastor in perhaps most churches, elders in some. What is seldom emphasized, though, is the New Testament expectation that maturity in all believers should qualify them to exercise an unofficial role of teaching/instructing/admonishing one another (Rom. 15:14; Col. 3:16). How are we to reconcile this with "not many should be teachers" (Jas. 3:1)? The same principle holds true for other spiritual gifts. Some have the gift of giving, but all believers are to give. Some have the gift of mercy, but all of us are to be merciful. Some have the gift of teaching, but all of us are to teach.

As with all other forms of one-anothering, teaching each other requires us to lay down our lives for our brothers and sisters. How? First, to be able to teach others requires competence. This takes a certain measure of discipline to learn the truth and how to express it in words others can understand and benefit from. Second, teaching—as a way of serving others—means unselfishly giving up some personal time and putting our own interests aside. Third, at times the truth that needs to be taught is not what others want to hear. In such cases, those doing the teaching must lay down their lives by risking disapproval.

Paul commended the believers in Rome for being "competent to instruct one another" (Rom. 15:14) and urged those in Colossae to "teach and admonish one another" (Col. 3:16). Countless believers, though, rarely if ever hear about this truth that we should all reach a point of being able to teach one another. Alongside this lack of emphasis runs the absence of opportunity to practice one-anothering through mutual teaching when we gather. From my years as a pastor I know it is much easier to do the teaching myself than to shape a meeting environment in which members of the body have the chance to grow in the experience of teaching one another.

A great many Christians today—even if they cannot articulate it—are seeking to return to the freedom and flexibility those first disciples experienced as they were learning from Jesus. In their book, *Church Refugees*, Josh Packard and Ashleigh Hope document the results of nearly a hundred conversations they had with the "dechurched," ranging in age from 18 to 84. The stories they heard came from "people who were disengaging with church but not with God."[2] One of those refugees, Emily, told them, "I've always had questions for the church, but there isn't much room in Christian churches and denominations to question."[3] The authors asked those they interviewed whether they thought Emily had a valid point. "The answer . . . was a resounding 'Yes!' They felt the ability to ask questions and explore various aspects of their faith wasn't supported in the church, and it was a major factor in their decisions to leave."[4] As the examples in the next chapter make clear, a congregational meeting can be structured in ways that allow questions, responses, and teaching by gifted teachers as well as by all believers.

Serving One Another

Like us, Jesus's first disciples preferred the catbird seat—which means, says Merriam-Webster, "a position of great prominence or advantage."[5] More than once those initial followers

---

[2] Packard and Hope, *Church Refugees,* 7.
[3] Ibid., 81.
[4] Ibid.
[5] *Merriam-Webster, s.v.* "catbird seat," accessed July 11, 2016, http://www.merriam-webster.com/dictionary/catbird%20seat.

of Jesus squabbled over which of them would get the top spots in his administration (Luke 9:46; 22:24). James and John even enlisted Mom in their bid for the most powerful posts in the coming Kingdom (Matt. 20:20). Years later, Diotrephes displayed the same appetite for outranking others (3 John 9). All of those early Christ-followers, as those subject to the Roman Empire, knew the score on what led to power and significance in that kingdom. Why would it be any different in the coming Kingdom of God?

In *Stewardship: Choosing Partnership Over Self-Interest*, Peter Block explains the desires behind both the drive to rule over and the willingness to be ruled:

> The expectations of dependency are that others will provide safety, freedom, and self-esteem. The expectations we have of dominance are that we are entitled to compliance, loyalty, and gratitude. These expectations . . . unstated emotional wants . . . have been traditionally evoked and agreed to each time we joined an institution. It didn't matter whether the institution was our family, school, work, or church. The institution wanted compliance and loyalty, and in return we wanted them to provide us with safety and self-esteem.[6]

Those in catbird seats measure their importance by the number of people who depend on them. The larger the kingdom, the greater the king. The one who gains the compliance and loyalty of a thousand is ten times more significant than the one with only a hundred conforming followers. The good life means having

---

[6] Block, *Stewardship,* 82.

others do for you. The distasteful life involves having to do for
others. Prominence and power make you into somebody; obscurity
and submissiveness . . . nobody.

Jesus, of course, flipped all these ideas over like hotcakes
on a griddle. What the disciples had known as "up" in the world
system would become "down" for those under the rule of the King
of Kings. "You know," he told them, "that the rulers of the Gentiles
lord it over them, and their high officials exercise authority over
them. Not so with you. Instead, whoever wants to become great
among you must be your servant" (Matt. 20:25-26). Jesus, of
course, demonstrated his own willingness to take the place of a
servant when he washed and toweled their feet.

And so one way to live out love for one another under the
new command of King Jesus is expressed in the subcommand to
"serve one another in love" (Gal. 5:13). Can Christ-followers be
given opportunities to practice serving each other in the setting
nearly everyone now calls church? Apparently so, judging by some
of the examples in Chapter Six.

Confessing Sins to One Another

When James instructed believers, "confess your sins to
each other" (5:16), he linked it with prayer for healing, and the
context speaks of calling for the elders of the church. There is no
New Testament command that would require anyone to stand
before a large assembly of believers to confess sinning. Luke
reports that new believers in Ephesus publicly confessed their sins
as they turned to Jesus (Acts 19:18). But we have no examples

from first-century churches in which Christians came before the entire church in confession.

Individually, of course, we are to confess our sins to God. And as James 5:16 makes clear, there is also a place for confessing our sins to other believers. This, says Dietrich Bonhoeffer, is "between two Christians. A confession of sin in the presence of all the members of the congregation is not required to restore one to fellowship with the whole congregation. I meet the whole congregation in the one brother to whom I confess my sins and who forgives my sins."[7]

That said, in rare cases publicly confessing sins may sometimes benefit both the one confessing as well as the congregation. In one church of about 150 people, the unmarried teenaged daughter of a prominent leadership couple became pregnant. When the young woman met with the pastor of the church, she acknowledged her action as wrong and was sincerely repentant. Although hers was a private sin, it had a public dimension and effect. Her father was serving as a church elder and her mother as a Sunday school teacher. Her pregnancy would, within a short time, become obvious to everyone in the congregation.

The pastor knew that unless this situation were dealt with properly, it could become the subject of whispered gossip. To forestall that, he met with the girl and her parents (the father-to-be was neither in the picture nor in the church). Would they agree,

---

[7] Dietrich Bonhoeffer, *Life Together: A Discussion of Christian Fellowship* (New York: Harper & Row, Publishers, 1954), 113.

the pastor asked, to having the girl stand with her parents before the congregation as she confessed before everyone, very simply and discreetly, what she had done? The request was simply made as an offer, without any kind of pressure or coercion. Although they found the decision difficult, all three saw the wisdom in doing so and agreed.

When the daughter stood before the church body, she did not go into any detail about her sin. She simply said that she had disobeyed God and that as a result of this had become pregnant. Abortion was out of the question. After her confession, the pastor invited any in the congregation who wished to assure her of their love and support to come forward and surround her as several prayed for her. She wept as perhaps three-quarters of those present came to the front and encircled her while a few offered prayers on her behalf.

The pastor reported that he heard not one word of gossip from anyone about the situation. The girl and her family knew that they were forgiven and accepted not only by God but also those in the congregation. Although no one will ever know, a likely additional effect took place in the hearts and minds of young people who saw this example of confession and restoration. Today, as an adult, the young woman who made the confession remains a part of the church.

The New Testament includes many more one-anothering instructions—each of them expanding on Jesus's new command. Most of them call for heart attitudes—ways to regard other believers: forgiving, accepting, honoring, agreeing with, bearing with, submitting to, and so on. But complying with the seven detailed in this chapter require observable outward actions that, in addition to engaging our hearts, also engage our bodies—mostly our hands and voices. All seven may be carried out when we gather, although doing so may require changes in the format and length of the meeting. All seven allow the body of Christ to grow and build itself in love "as each part does its work" (Eph. 4:16). Each of the seven actions is essential in full-fledged disciple-making. Chapter Six illustrates how more than a few churches are practicing these one-another commands in their main congregational meetings.

CHAPTER 6

One-Anothering in Churches

In this chapter, we have a spectrum of stories of leaders
who became intentional and put much effort in changing their
respective church paradigms into faith family gatherings where
God's work in individual lives is celebrated. While all these
stories are very different, there is a common thread of intimacy
with God bringing churches into a new paradigm of energizing
faith marked by vitality, vibrancy and meaning.
Healthy families share experiences in an open and
transparent way. Over the years of growing a family, a lot of time
is invested in getting things right and making the experiences
meaningful. But in our cities, many long for meaning to replace
the overabundance of shallow activity options.

Willy Kotiuga, Chair,
Bakke Graduate University Board of Regents

This very long chapter offers examples of how a variety of
churches are incorporating meaningful participation in their main
congregational meetings. Having served as a pastor for 21 years, I
know the pressures that tend to confine our perspective to the way
our church and others like ours do things. In this book you will
likely find approaches that differ from yours—and that is a healthy
discovery.

To each of the seven churches in the province of Asia,
Jesus—through John—sent a specific message relating to their

own circumstances. Every letter is unique, but in all seven Jesus included this identical sentence: "He who has an ear, let him hear what the Spirit says to the churches" (Rev. 2:7, 11, 17, 29; 3:6, 13, 22). That final word, *churches*, is plural. What we now know as the Book of Revelation, including all these letters, would have been read and heard in all seven churches. So each church had its own word from the Lord, but disciples with Spirit-tuned ears were to listen also to what he was saying to the other six.

Does Jesus still follow that pattern today? Is he calling each contemporary church to listen not only to what he is saying to it but also to learn from what he is saying to other churches about gathering practices? What the Spirit is saying to churches today should square with what he led the New Testament writers to record about church practice back then. Today the Church appears in many sizes and meets in a variety of settings. Any given assembly may number in the thousands, hundreds, or tens. Your church may meet in an elaborate building, a modest structure, a home, a garage, a workplace, or some other venue. Your locale may be urban, suburban, or rural.

Could it be that what the Spirit is saying to your church needs to be rounded out by what he is saying to others—just as those who first read or heard the seven letters received not only their own message but all those directed to the rest as well? Believing this to be the case, I am assuming in this book that whatever our church size, meeting place, or method, all of us need to learn from each other. This includes learning from churches in cultures and from traditions that differ from our own. The examples in these chapters have been drawn from a variety of backgrounds and customs for meeting together.

Church names, accompanied by locations, are listed in alphabetical order. The practice of each church may include one or more of the seven one-anothering actions described in Chapter Five. In the line following each church name, the bold-faced words highlight which of the seven figure most prominently in the narrative for that church.

Axiom Church, Syracuse, NY

| Greeting | Encouraging | Spurring On | **Teaching/Instructing** |
| Serving | Praying For | Confessing |

On its website, Axiom Church describes its city-renewal approach:

> Most churches revolve around a gifted preacher, a dynamic worship band and the race to grow as big as possible. In Axiom we've intentionally sought not to pursue that route.
>
> In 2010, four families took a big risk and moved from around the Northeast to root in Syracuse, NY. They intentionally slowed down to be present to each other and to the place they now lived. . . . Out of a desire to be deeply present on the Southwest side of Syracuse, Axiom has recently purchased a charming building that will host a space for public worship gatherings, a neighborhood coffee shop and opportunities to care for their under-resourced neighborhood.[1]

---

[1] "Our Story," Axiom, accessed May 7, 2016, http://axiomchurchny.com/about-us/our-story.

Curing Sunday Spectatoritis

For several years, Dan White preached monological sermons. In keeping with his training and experience in churches, he considered himself a platform preacher. "When I visualized what preaching is all about," he says, "it came down to me, a pulpit, and an audience. I relied heavily on my personality, my words, and my ability to bring the Word of God into focus for his people."[2]

But his concept of preaching began to change when White became a bivocational church planter. No longer working full-time on a church payroll, he did not have as much time for sermon preparation. The size of the congregation also made a difference. As he recalls, "It felt odd to preach monologically for 35 to 50 minutes with my spiritual family in the room."[3]

He began to look into some of the New Testament Greek words surrounding the preaching/teaching of Paul. "Most of his preaching," White says, "had an element of proclamation, but it was very dialogical. I began to realize that I had been interpreting what the New Testament said about preaching through my own contemporary lens."[4] This prompted him to wrestle with how to translate the way preaching was done in the first century into the twenty-first century context.

Today, White and the two other bivocational pastors in Axiom Church all practice a method of dialogical preaching that involves four "movements." This method addresses two legitimate fears about dialogical preaching—the dangers of (a) a meandering,

---

[2] Dan White, interview by author, November 19, 2015.
[3] Ibid.
[4] Ibid.

rudderless conversation and (b) a lack of authoritative proclamation. The four movements include:

Instructive

Dialogical preaching values declaring the Word of God with authority. So in this segment, the teacher speaks expositionally on a passage, without interruption, for 10 to 15 minutes. The text is explained in its historical and sociological context. Pressing truths are presented for the church family to wrestle with. This portion of the message contains no dialogue.

Before moving into the next stage, the teacher calls for a full minute of silence, asking the people to reflect on two questions about what they have just heard: (a) Where is there conflict for you? and (b) Where is there clarity for you? White learned the need for this silent period shortly after transitioning to dialogical preaching. If he moved immediately from proclamation to discussion, those with quick answers or who loved to talk dominated the conversation. This wait time levels the playing field by giving time for those who need time to process the truth just presented.

Expressive

Dialogical preaching values not only the declarative but also the discursive. White emphasizes it is not either/or but both/and. Here, the people are invited to respond to the two questions given during the wait time. The teacher, acting as moderator, draws out comments and assists in relating them to the theme of the message. The responses are sometimes personal, sometimes emotional. On occasion, a statement from someone in the congregation may contain even better insight into the text than what the teacher presented. If someone expresses a need for more clarity, the moderator may ask, "Can anyone else shed light on this question?" This segment takes 10 minutes.

Collective

For the next 5 minutes the teacher moves to a whiteboard, using it to collect significant insights and themes that emerged during the expressive period. Refinements take place in this section. For example, if the topic is love, and someone has said they used to think of love as a feeling, a few others may comment that love is work, requiring faithfulness. Main points from this interchange would get written onto the whiteboard.

Summarative (a made-up word)

This is given 10 minutes. Now the teacher, using material prepared beforehand, reconstructs the truth from the passage by pulling everything together. Relevant questions include: "What is God proclaiming over our lives?" "What is our take-home?" and "What should we stir on this week?" White says as his congregation has grown in dialogical experience, this section includes more and more of what is on the whiteboard. What people say in the *Expressive* segment lines up with what will be declared by the teacher in the *Summarative*.

Overall, the four movements of this dialogical method take from 40 to 45 minutes, of which more than half is declarative material prepared in advance by the teacher.

White and the other two pastors meet as a team each week to plan the dialogical message. Although only one of them will present it, the other two cross-pollinate by offering theological insights, sharing illustrations, suggesting approaches, and assessing the message from the previous week. This group process also allows them to include and coach potential teachers.

Those in Axiom Church have responded positively to dialogical preaching. For example, one woman told White, "In my previous church experience, I never felt I could offer any insights to the family of God—I was just consuming. Now I'm able to contribute. After a few months in Axiom Church, I began to realize my voice is heard here."[5] Agnostics can find places in the Axiom family dialogue, stating their questions honestly without having to hide. Dialogical preaching creates a missional space, conducive to those curious about Jesus. White says, "Many times I find that the most potent things are coming from the congregation. Lights come on when people hear another voice supplementing what the teacher is saying. It is a much richer environment."[6]

Whether the message is monological or dialogical, any teacher carefully crafts the sermon. But dialogical preaching, White contends, "brings it down to the bottom shelf. People will ask, 'Dan, are you saying . . . ?' In monological preaching, I would not be attuned to any confusion in the room. Now I'm far more aware of what people are not understanding. Before, I was a lot more concerned about my delivery of the message than its reception."[7]

What advice does White have for those wishing to transition to dialogical preaching? First, be prepared for a renovation of ego. "The first year," he admits, "my ego was taking a

---

[5] White, interview.
[6] Ibid.
[7] Ibid..

hit. I was defensive. Insecure. I seriously considered shutting down the dialogical journey. I was used to having 40 minutes of a perfectly crafted, uninterrupted, zinger of a message. Something in me had to die."[8]

Second, he recommends adopting a system for dialogical preaching. "If you wander into it, making conversation your only goal," he warns, "you will move toward chaos. But with a carefully thought-out system, it is not chaotic at all once you understand how to guide people into dialog."[9]

Now, after several years of dialogical preaching, White has become an enthusiastic proponent: "We need to create space for community. To hear the priesthood of believers amongst us. To introduce God's Word and go out with it."[10]

Bethany Baptist Church, Puyallup, WA

| Greeting | **Encouraging** | Spurring On | **Teaching/Instructing** |
| **Serving** | Praying For | Confessing |

While serving as pastor in Bethany Baptist, Lowell Bakke began to see a whole new way to make baptism an opportunity for those in the congregation to serve one another. As he explains it:

In those days I was baptizing around eight to ten people a year. Why, I wondered, should a pastor do all the baptizing? Jesus himself had his trainees baptize others (John 4:1-2).

---

[8] Ibid.
[9] Ibid.
[10] Ibid.

Apparently Paul did not consider baptizing disciples a part of his job description (1 Cor. 1:13-17).

As a Baptist pastor, I had no interest in claiming exclusive authority to baptize as a symbol of power, which is so common in Baptist churches. So I went to the church board and said, "I'd like to give away this responsibility to those who have actually done the ministry in the lives of those being baptized. Can you show me biblically that I am the only one who should do the baptizing?" They thought about it and said, "No—it's just that we've always done it that way."

Behind every baptism is a story of God's working, but I didn't want to be the one knowing and telling that story. So I began meeting with baptismal candidates, asking them to tell me their stories so they could tell them publically. Some needed a bit of coaching to help them know the best way to communicate their story publicly. "Who might you want to baptize you?" I asked each one. Usually it was the person who had had the most spiritual impact on their coming to faith. For some fathers, it was sometimes a child or wife who did the baptizing. Ballplayers baptized coaches. Students baptized teachers. In one case, an employee of a car company baptized the owner of the firm. But by far the most dynamic part of the service was the story of the relationship of those being baptized and the one who had the spiritual impact on their life.

In less than a year, the church witnessed more than 100 baptisms—and heard the story associated with each one. We actually had one Sunday morning where in three services all we did in each service was to hear the stories of people who were being baptized. Altogether 39 people were baptized that day, but it took the whole service time because each story was totally different. Twenty-plus years later, I don't remember all the stories, but I do remember thinking almost all of those who were baptized that day and every other baptismal service came to Christ outside our church services. Had we not taken the time to learn and share the story, we would never had known how God was working the other six days of the week in Puyallup.

Formerly, believers at Bethany took seriously the responsibility for bringing people to Christ, but the church did not give them the opportunity to share their story nor the authority to baptize those they reached on behalf of the church. Now they were out sharing Christ in the community and had the opportunity to tell their stories to church body as well as the joy of representing the church as the baptizing agent in the church service. Those stories were better than any sermon I ever preached.

For three summers while serving as pastor in in this church, I used a five-question strategy. This not only increased participation among those who had gathered each Sunday, but it also helped vacationing church members take part. Maybe the best part of the whole process was that it put everyone on an equal footing—young believers, mature believers, and not-yet-believers—as every person's answers were valuable to the whole. I chose a Bible book and divided it into sections. Each section became my text for that week, and everyone was notified in advance of the Scripture passage to be read. To vacationers I suggested, even if you're camping, take out this text and read it carefully. Then ask yourself the following five questions:

What did you like about this text?

What did you not like about the text?

What did you not understand about the text?

What did you learn about God—Father, Son, Holy Spirit?

What are you going to do now that you've read the text?

For the message in the Sunday meeting, I began by asking others to read the text aloud in two or three translations. After that I presented a short teaching commentary on the text then asked those present to interact, using the same five questions. Roving microphones made it possible for everyone to hear clearly. I was amazed at some of the insights. It made me realize that even with the aid of the Holy Spirit, my mind as a pastor is so finite that I don't understand many things about the Bible that the congregation was able to bring to the table each Sunday.

When it came to questions 1 and 2, what some people liked about the text was sometimes identical with what others did not like about it, depending on their perspective and their circumstances in life. When people described what they did not understand about the text (question 3), I did not offer answers. Often, a week or two later, someone would say something like, "I remember last week when John was struggling to understand the text. Well, while reading this week's Scripture the Lord helped me see something I think might help with that." The hardest thing for preachers is to refrain from giving answers. We need to trust the Holy Spirit to teach believers as they work their way through to understanding.[11]

Christ Church Deal, Deal, Kent, UK

| Greeting | Encouraging | Spurring On | **Teaching/Instructing** |
| Serving | Praying For | Confessing |

Both Eph. 5:19 and Col. 3:16 associate singing with speaking to one another and teaching each other. Often, though, the congregational focus is less on "one another" than on the vocal

---

[11] Lowell Bakke, interview by author, July 30, 2015.

and instrumental musicians up front. In this excerpt from *Trinity in Human Community*, Peter Holmes describes what Christ Church Deal has done to shift the focus back to one-anothering.

> Another change in our own community was when we moved the worship band to the back of the congregation, requiring each person to proactively visualize worshipping Christ in relationship rather than continue to be passively "led" in worship by the singers and musicians. This change has also allowed the singers and musicians to be more part of the body of worshippers (e.g. on the same level, rather than at the altar or on stage in front of everyone). It is an attempt to mirror social Trinity by a visual declaration of openness and relational oneness. This had not necessarily improved the quality of the worship time, or been helpful for everyone. Most of us in the congregation would agree that when it comes to sung worship on Sundays, we still have a long way to go. But this idea has changed the focus and is one of the first things that visitors from other churches comment on.[12]

Church for Men, an Online Blog

| Greeting | Encouraging | Spurring On | **Teaching/Instructing** |
| Serving | Praying For | Confessing |

On his website, Church for Men, David Murrow describes a discovery he made through leading retreats for men. Clearly the group dynamics in a men's retreat differ greatly from those in a church service. But it is worth asking: How can what Murrow has

---

[12] Holmes, *Trinity in Human Community*, 41.

learned be adapted to the teaching that takes place on Sunday morning? (The following is excerpted from Church for Men.)

The average man can pay close attention to a monologue lecture for about 10 minutes. After that his mind will tend to wander.

A few years ago, after *Why Men Hate Going to Church* hit the bookshelves, I began speaking to groups. I did the usual: talk for 40 minutes. It wasn't long before I noticed men dropping off after 12 minutes or so. I thought I was a bad speaker—until I looked around during other presenters' talks and noticed the same thing happening. Ditto during sermons at church.

So I decided to try something different. *If guys pay close attention for ten minutes, then that's how long I'll teach.* I designed a retreat weekend around a 10-10 teaching format.

The first thing I do is put the guys into small discussion teams of 2, 3 or 4. Then I speak for 10 minutes. Next, I project questions on a screen. Each team takes 10 minutes to discuss the questions. Then I teach 10 more minutes, and so on.

The 10-10 format breaks up the teaching and gives men more opportunities to get to know one another. Here's what I've learned about the 10-10 format:

The number of men who nod off or check their phones has decreased by 80%.

The amount of table talk has doubled.

Men pay closer attention to what I'm saying because they know talk time is coming and they have to be ready to answer the questions.

Everyone gets a chance to participate.

Men regularly tell me my retreats are the best ever, even though I talk much less than the average retreat speaker.

Men have more opportunities to build friendships.

Let me comment on that last point: guys can get great teaching anywhere. But friendships are hard to come by.

Jesus told his disciples to love one another. The 10-10 format gives men an opportunity to share their stories, get to know one another and support one another. The 10-10 format is designed to build friendships, particularly if you assign guys to groups of three and ask them to sit together every week.

The monologue model sends a powerful message: you are here to receive information from an expert. The 10-10 model sends a different message: you are here to be known and loved.[13]

Community Church of Hayward, CA

| Greeting | Encouraging | Spurring On | Teaching/Instructing |
| **Serving** | Praying For | Confessing |

Marilyn Bennet, equipping pastor of Community Church, describes how serving each other through meals transformed life for everyone in this church, including those who had previously hurried home after the Sunday meeting.

Several years ago we began to serve lunch right after our morning church service by extending the church potluck on the first Sunday of the month into a weekly luncheon. We were fortunate we always had members who wanted to prepare and clean up. We have had international theme lunches but have been most successful with a variety of choices for sandwiches, salads,

---

[13] David Murrow, "Use the 10-10 Format to Teach Men," *Patheos* (blog), accessed April 7, 2016, http://www.patheos.com/blogs/churchformen/2015/06/use-the-10-10-format-to-teach-men/.

and desserts. If someone has a birthday, they bring their own cake to celebrate. Every Sunday our fellowship leader asks people to sign up to bring their deli choices for the next Sunday. Initially not all of our members would remember, so one lady took it upon herself to call those who signed up.

At first our attendees rushed home after church. Gradually some stayed for lunch. This change took years to become the norm. Now people are staying until 4 or 5 o'clock, making the weekly luncheon a meaningful part of church life. What has developed is not only closer relationships between parishioners, but also a closer relationship between our four pastors and our parishioners.[14]

Elim Evangelical Free Church, Puyallup, WA

| Greeting | Encouraging | Spurring On | **Teaching/Instructing** |
| Serving | **Praying For** | Confessing |

Elim traces its roots back more than a century, to January 12, 1884, when a small group of believers gathered in a home in Tacoma, Washington. The church met in various places in Tacoma over the years, then moved into its present building on South Hill, Puyallup, in the 1970s. Here—in the Sunday morning gathering— members of the congregation may ask questions and support one another in prayer. The following is based on an interview with Martin Schlomer, pastor.

----

[14] Marilyn Bennet, e-mail message to author, July 23, 2015.

Curing Sunday Spectatoritis

From time to time, following a sermon Schlomer opens a time for questions and answers. If he himself is to respond to what is being asked, he is more comfortable with subjects he knows well. On other topics, he sometimes asks a knowledgeable panel to be ready to reply to the questions. He may ask panel members to join him up front or to speak into a roving microphone from their places in the congregation.

Recently Schlomer began inviting people to text their questions to him on the spot. He now regrets agreeing to allow the questions to be sent anonymously. Without knowing who has asked the question, he has found it difficult to put the question into context.

Not regularly, but perhaps once a month, Schlomer structures an opportunity for those in the congregation to pray for one another. He sometimes introduces this special time after teaching on a Scripture passage such as 1 Peter 5:7, "Cast all your anxiety on him because he cares for you." Or when the church has a prayer time not associated with the message, he does not teach on the Scripture but offers a couple of reflections that people will identify with in their experience.

He might ask something like, "How many of you are dealing with cares this morning?" As people respond with raised hands, he then invites others to move beside them and to say, "May I pray for you?" Schlomer says he has never had any objections from people who have been prayed for. However, he admits that these prayer times are uncomfortable for some, so it is always presented as a completely voluntary ministry. No one is put on the spot.

On some Sundays, Schlomer asks those who want to be prayed for to write out their requests, pin them to a wall, and stand beside them. Others are then invited to join those by the wall and pray for them. Normally this time of praying for each other continues for 10 to 15 minutes.[15]

First Covenant Church of St. Paul, St. Paul, MN

| Greeting | **Encouraging** | **Spurring On** | Teaching/Instructing |
| **Serving** | **Praying For** | Confessing |

This 141-year-old church, situated in a community that struggles economically, is passionately intercultural, intergenerational, and participatory on Sunday mornings. These characteristics matured in response to the neighborhood surrounding its building. Decades ago First Covenant decided to stay put instead of exiting to the suburbs. An elementary school lies just across the street from its building, a high school sits on an opposite corner, and a middle school is an easy quarter-mile walk away. The following is based on an interview with Anne Vining, pastor.

When Vining came on board as pastor in 2002, the school already had a strong relationship with the elementary school and its principal. Although located in a financially disadvantaged area, the school was thriving thanks to this man who did everything possible to afford opportunities and resources for students. Part of those resources have come from First Covenant, which provides

---

[15] Martin Schlomer, interview by author, August 27, 2015.

space when the school needs it. The church also offers afterschool programming in which kids can come across the street after school for tutoring, creative arts, and meals.

Ten years ago the church hired a worship and arts minister from Argentina who had experience in directing musicals. They began putting on Christmas musicals that included interested kids from the neighborhood schools. This ministry expanded until now they are putting on Broadway musicals, including *Les Misérables, Fiddler on the Roof,* and *Annie.* These include about 40 students from the three schools plus another 40 children and young people from the church. Weekend musicals draw audiences of 900 to 1000.

While respecting the separation of church and state, the church, through the musicals, has been able to build relationships with the students. These friendships grow as the church provides meals, transportation, guitar and drum lessons, and other training in the creative arts. Out of the 250-300 church members who attend on a typical Sunday, nearly half of them are involved in this musical ministry with students from these neighborhood schools.

Sunday services reflect the servant hearts and the close ties the adults in First Covenant have formed with children and young people. When a child reaches the seventh grade, he or she is paired with an adult prayer partner. Young people participate in worship teams. High schoolers, alongside adults, take part in serving Communion. Scripture-reading teams of two are always intergenerational and intercultural.

A gospel choir, which sings every three or four weeks, includes all ages—from kindergarteners to seniors in their 80s. In their practices, the older ones hear prayer requests from the younger ones—and vice versa—and they all discuss what the song means.

Several years ago a girl came into First Covenant through taking part in one of the musicals. She grew up, married, and gave birth to a blind daughter. Her husband, a recovering alcoholic, recently shared a powerful testimony of how coming to faith has given him strength in battling his addiction. In her own testimony, the woman told the church how, while listening to a song about being fearfully and wonderfully made, she knew her daughter would be born blind. One Sunday morning that daughter, who is the family's spiritual leader, read the parable of the sower—reading with her hands from her Braille Bible. This brought the entire congregation to tears.

Vining says "it takes a ton of time to live into" the vision of an intergenerational, intercultural, participatory church. But she clearly believes it is time well invested.[16]

Grace Community Church, Gresham, OR

| Greeting | **Encouraging** | **Spurring On** | **Teaching/Instructing** |
| Serving | Praying For | Confessing |

In the following account, Bob Maddox and Dena Stuerhoff tell how they are making their main congregational meetings (now three per Sunday) participative. Bob oversees assimilation and small groups. Dena serves as office manager. They were eager to talk about this subject.

---

[16] Anne Vining, interview by author, November 5, 2015.

Bob: We're incredibly passionate about empowering our people. When something needs to happen, our first thought is to look to members of the body and ask, "Who can do that?" Do we want the professionals up front all the time? Or do we want to empower the people to do the work of ministry? We aim for the latter choice. Rather than killing ourselves as pastors trying to do all the work, we become coordinators of people.

One of our pastors can get up and say, "We're going to have Tom come up and illustrate this point." Suddenly, the mood in the entire auditorium changes. Everyone stops and leans forward, wanting to hear Tom's story. In reality, the average person's story grabs people. It is able to penetrate and cut through some of the hardness our culture has built into us. It also cuts through the ways we have conditioned ourselves not to listen when someone is preaching. We choose to have people from the body up front on a fairly regular basis, because they can say things we staff people cannot.

Dena: We just had our Missions Sunday. Bob taught for about 17 minutes, but the bulk of the content came from people sharing. When a team returns from a mission trip, we ask them to come and report to the congregation. The same goes for community work days, cleanup and repair efforts at schools. Those who took part come up and tell about their experience.

Bob does a lot of work to help people prepare. Speaking up front is terrifying for some. They would rather go out of the country than to speak in public. Bob does a great job of equipping or, as he likes to say, coaching them. He might suggest narrowing their comments down to three points. He or another staff person will meet with them and let them practice. We don't spring the speaking request on them the night or the Friday beforehand. If at all possible, they know weeks in advance.

Bob: Churches typically do either of two things. Some never let anyone speak up front. Others put them up there with no coaching. That doesn't go well, and so they say let's not do that again. We are convinced that the people can tell the story far better than we can. What they say will penetrate far better, because—unlike us pastors—they are not being paid to speak. Even if they stumble and fumble, people will still listen. We've got to let the body be involved with the body. We need to believe in our people—but help them with coaching

Dena: We regularly schedule baptisms. Beforehand, though, those being baptized meet with a pastor and share their testimony privately before they do so publicly. Coaching, again, happens at this point. In addition to speaking their testimony publicly, we ask them to write it out. Then we publish it in the bulletin and include it along with printed sermons. In this way, others may both hear and read the person's story of how they came to the point of baptism.

Bob: Fairly often, at the end of a sermon series, people will have questions that the teaching has raised but not answered. So we will form a panel of, say, three persons up front. Then we open things up for questions from the body. This usually makes up the entire service.

Dena: Sometimes we will provide a text number and invite people to text their questions right on the spot to one of the pastors during the sermon. Increasingly, we're trying to incorporate technology.[17]

---

[17] Bob Maddox, Dena Stuerhoff, interview by author, September 3, 2015.

Curing Sunday Spectatoritis

Jacob's Well Church, Chicago, IL

| Greeting | **Encouraging** | **Spurring On** | **Teaching/Instructing** |
| Serving | Praying For | Confessing |

On their website, this church describes its participative Sunday meetings: "We believe that worship services should not be passive experiences, and the congregation should not be simply 'audience members.' We are a community. We provide a time in the service to talk and ask questions. We sit around tables. We drink coffee. We take notes, and we ask questions."[18] After seminary, Mark Brouwer planted churches in Austin, TX and Minneapolis, MN, then spent a few years in recovery ministry and coaching pastors. He has been serving as pastor in Jacob's Well Church since 2011. In the following interview, he answers several questions on how they counteract congregational passivity.

What led you to a participatory approach on Sundays?

One reason I wanted to serve in Jacob's Well was that for several years before my arrival the church had already been combining teaching and discussion. During the years I worked in the recovery arena and coached other pastors, I had been leading workshops and speaking at conferences. In most of those venues, we had a Q & A time after I spoke. Also, as I visited churches during that period, I discovered how strange it was to sit through a service as a passive observer. I came to believe including discussion times is more biblical and helpful to spiritual growth.

---

[18] "Who We Are," Jacob's Well Chicago, accessed April 11, 2016, http://www.jacobswellchicago.com/#/different/.

Although the conversational method drew me to the church, I did undergo an adjustment period. At first I tried to figure out what my predecessor had been doing and to follow suit. He had completely intermingled his teaching with congregational discussion. I found, though, that this did not work for me. So I said, let me just give a message and have discussion afterward. And the church agreed.

What does the Sunday meeting format look like at Jacob's Well?

Our meetings run from 10:00 to 11:30 a.m. We all sit at small tables in groups of four or five. The meeting begins with singing a few songs together, followed by conversation at the table. I usually provide three questions to guide the discussions. The first is designed to help those at each table to get to know each other better and relate to the sermon. The second might be: What are you thankful for this week? And the third: "What would you like others to pray for this week?" I sometimes suggest that the person sitting closest to the projection screen start the discussion. This period continues for just over 10 minutes. A countdown timer on the screen helps the table groups use the time effectively. Someone at each table closes this time in prayer. We then break for five minutes for coffee and snacks.

When we regroup, I spend the next 30 minutes or so presenting a sermon I've prepared. During the message, I refer back to the questions everyone has discussed at their table. A 15-minute, congregation-wide discussion follows the sermon. We always have a "runner" with a roving microphone so that everyone can hear and comments may be recorded. Anyone may offer a reflection, add a thought, or ask a question. This is a casual time in which we welcome new ideas, affirmations, and conflicting opinions. I wrap up the morning with a closing prayer. People then stay as long as they wish for additional fellowship.

Any lessons from your experience with combining the sermon with discussion?

Just as conventional preaching requires art and skill, so does preaching with dialogue. Someone may offer a comment you don't entirely agree with. In some cases, the remark may be completely errant. Or people may push back against something you said in your message. You need to learn how to deal tactfully and gracefully with situations like that.

In the beginning I had to learn how not to let the congregation treat me like the Bible answer-person. I have a lot to say, so my default is always to answer the question! At first, I tried to forestall this by inviting a panel to join me up front—a seminary student and a member of our leadership board. After I finished the sermon, each of them would have an opportunity to say something before we opened it up for questions from the congregation. However, that soon became too cumbersome, and we discontinued it. Now, I simply try to discipline myself not to answer immediately so that the dialogue may continue.

Sometimes the discussion can devolve into people merely saying what they like about the message. It's a bit like watching a movie with others, then simply talking about the movie afterward. To keep this from happening, I always come prepared with a couple of questions to help people focus on the issues. Most of the time, though, the discussions stay on track without the questions.

You are enthusiastic about preaching that includes discussion. Why?

Doing it this way has shattered some of my preconceptions. For example, in my experience churches can be nervous about having guest speakers or allowing members of the congregation to tell their stories. The worrisome question is: What if they say something that is off base? But when you begin having open discussions, all this becomes much easier. If a comment does not pass biblical muster, it will get corrected in the Q and A time. Our leaders, in fact, see this as part of their role. This creates a lot more freedom in bringing people in from outside the church. If it is not said perfectly, it will still work itself out.

A common assumption about discussions in the Sunday meetings concerns visitors. Will they be afraid to speak up because they are newcomers? Will they be put off? I have found just the opposite to be true. More often than not visitors will be the first to ask questions or make comments. The less church background people have, the more likely they are to speak up.

So, yes, I am enthusiastic about Sunday morning dialogue. I believe this would work, to some degree, whatever the size of the church.

How else are you making Jacob's Well meetings more participatory?

Our pastor-intern and I and divide our time between Jacob's Well and another church about 30 minutes away. At each church, he speaks once and I speak twice per month. On the first Sunday of the month, the other church has a potluck brunch, while Jacob's Well holds its brunch on the last Sunday.

On Brunch Sunday we sing and eat together, but there is no preaching. After the meal we discuss a variety of topics. Quite often someone will share for five to seven minutes. They may tell how God is working in their families, neighborhoods, or workplaces. Discussion of what they have said follows. When someone brings a faith story, others respond not simply with questions but with affirmations. This is a powerful way for the members of the body to validate each other.

All in all, participatory church meetings have made it clear that there is a lot of wisdom in this church—far more than just what I am able to bring.[19]

The Kingdom Citizens' Pavilion, Jos, Nigeria

| Greeting | Encouraging | **Spurring On** | **Teaching/Instructing** | | **Serving** | **Praying For** | Confessing |

On their website, Dotun Reju, founding pastor, writes that this church aims "to bring saints to perfection fully equipped and prepared for the work of the ministry with the sole intent of wielding great influence in social, economic and political spheres of Nigeria and in the nations of the world."[20] Nigeria is classified as a nation that constitutes a risk to the civilized world. In the same his article, "The Politics of Terrorism," Reju writes, "The spate of religious crises has continued unabated in the country. As I write this piece, my city, Jos is still observing curfew from midnight to six a.m. since November 2008 as a result of religious riots."[21] The following description of how this church prepares its young people for the work world is adapted from a written "Report on KCP Invaders Induction Ceremony"[22] provided by Reju.

---

[19] Mark Brouwer, interview by author, February 5, 2016.

[20] "About Us: Our Vision," The Kingdom Citizens' Pavilion, accessed April 11, 2016, http://www.thekingdomcitizensng.com/our-vision/.

[21] Dotun Reju, "The Politics of Terrorism," accessed July 11, 2016, http://pastordot.blogspot.com/2010/01/politics-of-terrorism.html

[22] Dotun Reju, message to author, September 9, 2015.

Twice a year, during its Sunday morning service, this church commissions young people to serve Christ in their prospective workplaces. Well in advance of this day, the church identifies all upcoming graduates from colleges and vocational training centers and invites them to become part of the Invaders Squad. Students who join complete a series of seminars and workshops that equip them with a biblical understanding of working in the world as a Christian. Each is assigned a mentor to assist in preparing them for the next stage of life.

To become a part of the squad, candidates must subscribe to a pledge that reads, in part, as follows:

1. To display excellence in my work as befits a minister of the gospel.

2. To be committed to accountability by submitting to a deliberate mentoring process in the discharge of my God-ordained assignment.

3. To commit to the passionate pursuit of these goals until it becomes the governing principle in my sphere of influence.

4. I acknowledge that this God-beloved world is darkened by the agenda of unscrupulous and perverted men, and that God desires men and women to partner with Him in restoring His government.

5. I hereby declare my unalloyed allegiance to His divine call and offer my life, talent, gifting and professional training as tools of Kingdom advancement by setting His standards in the midst of the widespread perversion.

6.　　　I elect to illuminate mankind with the glory of God's kingdom of righteousness, peace, and joy. I pledge in all seasons to show my loyalty to the Most High, who still declares "Let there be light."[23]

On commissioning Sunday, all the candidates march into the auditorium in procession with a hymn. This is followed by Bible reading and a charge. As each stands before the congregation, the mentor presents him or her with a citation. This is followed as they all make their pledges. After this, they kneel for prayers of consecration. After prayer, they rise and are decorated by the leader of the squad. Alumni squad members then embrace them and welcome them with handshakes. A church dinner that includes community leaders climaxes the commissioning service.

Ene Obaje, one of the squad members now in the work world, describes her experience in these words:

Before my induction as an invader, I had attended about two sessions of theology of work. This gave me insight on how to live and work with godly perspective, but I never completely felt responsible about a lot of things even though I was conscious of them. But after going through the induction process . . . I realized there was more to it, I became very deliberate about all I did (both business and personal life). I became conscious of the world around me and reminded myself daily that I have to set a pace for others to follow in the business world.

---

[23] Ibid.

So far it's not been easy because I get tempted to satisfy my flesh occasionally, but when I receive compliments about my product and advice on sticking to the standard, I feel really blessed and encouraged to do better. I know I have been able to come this far because I chose to do right no matter the cost, and I know that was what I signed in for. I am still praying for strength to carry on because I am just starting and believe there are more challenges and temptations ahead. But with what I know now and who I have become, I believe am going to get better in professing Christ daily in my work place as I grow.[24]

Lacey Presbyterian Church, Lacey, WA

| Greeting | **Encouraging** | **Spurring On** | **Teaching/Instructing** |
| Serving | Praying For | **Confessing** |

Think of the spurring on that could take place upon hearing an account like the following presented during a Sunday morning meeting in this church. In a segment called Sharing in the Spirit, a couple we'll call Brett and Susan spoke for 5 minutes. They began by saying that they saw Genesis 1 and 2 as making it clear that one of our core callings is to build community. The following is a transcript of what they shared with the congregation in the summer of 2015.

Brett: When Susan and I moved into our cul-de-sac in August of 1993, ours was the first house there. As other houses were built and people moved in, we made it our goal to be salt and light in the new neighborhood. So we made it a point to

---

[24] Ibid.

welcome and befriend each new family. We also began making it a practice in our morning devotional time together to pray around the cul-de-sac for each person by name. We still do this, not every day, but frequently.

Susan: Two decades plus is a long time, but let me mention a few things I remember about how we've been able to show the love of God to our neighbors. We've invited them in for dinner or sometimes for Italian sodas. I've had women over for backyard tea parties. Over the years, we have taken part in wedding receptions for the children of neighbors. Two have died since we've lived here, and we attended their memorial services. I've done babysitting for young mothers. Last year we flew to Hawaii to be part of the marriage ceremony for a couple who had moved from our cul-de-sac. We've shared garden produce. For several years we coordinated neighborhood barbecues, but this year some younger families are stepping into this role.

Brett: Over the years, the Lord has opened several ways to bear witness to our faith. Our next-door neighbors, who had been hurt in another church, began participating in a Tuesday evening Bible study in our home. We have also invited families to join us for Thanksgiving and Christmas events at church—and they have done so.

A military wife came to Susan one day and said her six-year-old had some questions about God. So she brought the little girl and we spent time talking with her. As a result of this, we purchased a copy of *The Story* for them. Since then, the mother has indicated that she has been reading from it to her three girls. The military husband of this woman is being sent to Germany, and the wife is having difficulty getting her passport. We promised to pray for her.

Susan: The ages in our neighborhood range from nearly 2 to 75 years. Six out of nine of the residents have lived here the entire 22 years we've been at this address. Several different nationalities are represented, as well as several different church affiliations as well as those with no organized church connections.

I've loved the sense of community that God has given us here. For example, this summer there have been spontaneous games of badminton in the street—with the majority of the homes participating. We have six little children at the moment, and it's fun to see them roller-blading, bike-riding, and driving their motorized vehicles up and down our driveway.

Brett: Later today, at 1:30 p.m., we will join our neighbors for a farewell barbecue for the military family moving to Germany. A couple of weeks ago, Susan and I decided to gather information from and take photos of each family in the cul-de-sac for a Shutterfly book to present to them. Here is the book. It contains names, snail mail addresses, email addresses, and phone numbers. Each household also wrote a personal message to the military family, who plan to rent out their house and return after three years.

So God has answered our prayers for community and for opportunities to be salt and light in our cul-de-sac. Susan and I are grateful to have had this opportunity.[25]

After they finished with this report on their neighborhood ministry, someone remarked, "Don't you wish we all lived in Brett's and Susan's cul-de-sac?"

On a Sunday during the same summer, in another Sharing in the Spirit segment, a woman named Taffy confessed how God worked to deliver her from wrong attitudes that had ruined the

---

[25] "Brett" and "Susan," transcript provided to author, June 15, 2015.

relationship with her mother. The following is a transcript of her presentation.

My name is Taffy and I have been asked to talk about how God's upper story has unfolded in the lower story of my life. Well, much is yet to be revealed, but I do see God's upper story in one place in my lower story now, that being in the care of my mother.

We have been attending Lacey Presbyterian Church since 1996, so many of you here today have seen this story unfolding and have been a big part of it. Many of you heard me say, more than once, I could never take care of Mom. I am so grateful for my sister. She took care of Mom until my sister died last year.

Mom and I did not get along when I was a child. This is partly because we are much the same. It is also because God gave me an intellect, some opportunities and a little talent that made me think life was all about me. This pride and selfishness in my personality caused great conflict in my relationship with my mom.

Fortunately, God also gave me a willing and teachable spirit and provided a godly grandmother and a father with a servant's heart as well as mentors, Bible studies, scriptures and teachings, wise friends, and examples of godly servants. I knew I wanted to be more like Jesus, so I asked.

It took a long time, but God provided people and circumstance to chip away at that pride and selfishness. Like:

The junior high teacher who happened to meet me in the hallway in my freshman year of high school and say, "Did you get mad when you got one B on your report card?"

The college teacher who said I used the word I too many times in my letter of interest.

Coworkers who did not include me in work activities.

Bosses who did not give me credit for the work I created.

Husband who has a higher IQ than I have.

Children who would say, "Mom please don't sing so loud."

Daughter who wanted to handle the planning of her own wedding and did not want my help.

Son who would say, "Mom, you are acting like a child and I already have two children. I don't need three children."

Granddaughter who says, "Grandma, are you seriously going to wear that?"

Fellow musicians who said I had too much vibrato in my voice, or was not in tune, or too loud, or not blending, etc.

Session members who said other church projects or programs were more important than those I considered needed.

A dear aunt who was willing to tell me a couple of times, "This is not the time or place to talk about that."

Congregation members who said I needed to talk less to make my point.

All of these remarks hurt at the time but, like Joseph in the book of Genesis, I can say they were for my good.

Because when the right time came, and enough of that selfishness and pride had been chipped away, God gave me the privilege of having Mom near me to get to know better.

Now I am learning to know Mom in a new way and actually enjoying spending time with her, and I thank God that he faithfully continues the work he began in me.[26]

---

[26] "Taffy," transcript provided to author, January 7, 2016.

A conversation in an adult Sunday school class led to the creation of a video that Stuart Dugan, pastor, included during the church's main weekly meeting.

During discussion in class, "Bob" told of how God had made a way through a workplace crisis. After class, he agreed to be interviewed in a video recording for use in the church service. In the video, he told how he had been supervising about 20 people in a major telecommunications company. The difficulty began when he was asked to oversee more than 40 who were working three shifts around the clock. He soon discovered one shift was full of bitter employees who came to view him more as an enemy than as a friend. Over the next two years, he often received harassing phone calls in the middle of the night. Worn down, he felt completely overwhelmed. "One day," he said, "at my desk in front of everyone, not really caring about what people thought, I just bowed my head and asked God to take the burden."[27]

"Immediately," he said, "the burden was lifted and I felt this warmth around me. For a moment I lost all sense of what was going on around me and was just hearing this calm voice."[28] When he got up from his desk, he knew that he needed to make the decision to get out of management and return to the regular work force.

What did he learn from this experience? "That God is there with us 24-7," he said, "whether we realize it or not."[29] Later, seeing the change in him, a couple of people came up to him to ask

---

[27] "Bob," conversation with author, September 6, 2015.
[28] Ibid.
[29] Ibid.

him to explain. Bob believes God may have used this in drawing them to Christ.

Dugan used this 4-minute video as part of his sermon in the church service on Labor Day. His text was Colossians 3:22 – 4:1, in which Paul addressed Christian slaves/employees in the first century. After the service "Joan," a woman from the congregation approached someone in tears expressing gratitude for the video. Through the sermon and hearing Bob's story, God had lifted a work-burden from her. Joan, who works for a government agency, had been dealing with a claimant who is a known drug felon. "I was judging her," Joan admitted. "After the claimant's attorney contacted me, I wrote an angry, stinging letter—and immediately regretted it after sending it. That night, Friday, I could not sleep and was miserable all through Saturday."[30]

Then, on Sunday, she heard the Labor Day sermon. What especially spoke to her were the words from Colossians 3:25: "Anyone who does wrong will be repaid for his wrong, and there is no favoritism." The pastor explained that since God will take care of those who need to be punished, we can leave that to him without trying to do it ourselves. She also listened as Bob told his story on video. "It is so emotional," she said, "when your peers tell what is going on in their lives."[31]

And then? "I left that church meeting in tears—but with a heart so light I couldn't believe the change. When I return to work

[30] "Joan," conversation with author, September 6, 2015.
[31] Ibid.

I will call the attorney and say I should not have written that letter."[32]

A few days later Joan said she had indeed called the attorney, who said the drug charge had been hanging over the claimant since her conviction as a teenager. Now, though, the woman is working hard to change her lifestyle and has served as a caregiver for more than 15 years.

Mill City Church, Minneapolis, MN

| Greeting | Encouraging | Spurring On | Teaching/Instructing |
| Serving | Praying For | Confessing |

Planted in 2009 and meeting in Sheridan School, Mill City Church has discovered a variety of creative ways to incorporate one-anothering. Stephanie Williams, who shares the lead-pastor role with Michael Binder, says the congregation numbers about 450, with a turnout of about 250 on a typical Sunday. The following is based on an interview with Stephanie Williams.

The weekly gathering begins with a "community time" in which people are encouraged to get to know someone they have not met before. Regulars are encouraged to find a new face. This segment is always introduced with two suggested questions to help conversations get underway. First question: "What brought you to Mill City?" The second question is intentionally worded to work even if the parties are complete strangers. For example, "What is your favorite fall activity?" Sometimes it is linked to the sermon

---

[32] Ibid.

topic. For example, if the message will cover what Scripture says about listening, the question might be: "Who is the best listener you know?" The leaders try to avoid any question that might cause anyone discomfort. To make it meaningful, the community time lasts from five to eight minutes (in contrast to the 60 seconds or so often given to a greeting time). As Stephanie puts it, "You can't remember someone unless they share something with you."[33]

Mill City Church has devised a number of ways for people to serve each other by communicating both what they need and what they have to offer. One method involves a bulletin board divided into two halves. One side is labeled: "I Have," the other, "I Need." Topics cover the waterfront. The "haves" might include a car-seat outgrown by a child, a used car, or a twin bed. "Need" items have included everything from babysitters to jobs to recommendations for plumbers. The church also maintains an online version of the bulletin board on Facebook.

Four times each year Mill City Church schedules what they call Training Sundays. Instead of staying in the main meeting room, those in the congregation may choose one of four different locations. The idea is to provide people an opportunity to actually do what they are being taught, to practice what they have just discussed. For example, when the theme was prayer, one group focused on spiritual warfare, another on healing, and a third on doing prayer walks in the neighborhood (they actually went out into the neighborhood surrounding the school building and did a prayer walk). Those who may not be comfortable with this have

---

[33] Stephanie Williams, interview by author, October 18, 2015.

the option of joining a fourth group and staying in the main room for a meeting much like a typical Sunday gathering. On the prayer-emphasis Sunday, they heard a message on the Lord's Prayer, ending by reciting it together. "Most enjoy having a choice," Stephanie recalls. "Rather than asking people to come out for training in another meeting, we want to provide this hands-on experience right on a Sunday morning. If we were to have scheduled prayer training at some other time, say on an evening, we probably would not even see 30 people show up."[34]

Contact cards are provided each week. Staff members regularly tell the congregation that they want to hear what God is doing in the lives of the people. By filling in a card and dropping it into the offering basket, those in the congregation can alert the staff to significant stories. Any card may generate an invitation to speak to the congregation during the announcement or sharing time. These may involve a live or video-recorded interview. Some tell their stories as sermon applications. "We talk a lot about how God is moving in neighborhoods and workplaces," Stephanie says. "Our congregation loves the workplace stories. We will soon be starting a sermon series on living out faith at work."[35]

Stephanie and Michael usually preach on alternate Sundays, with an associate pastor speaking every six weeks or so. Here, too, they seek to make their messages participatory. For example, in a message on discernment, those in the congregation were given post-it notes and asked to write out in about 3 minutes

---

[34] Ibid.
[35] Ibid.

what they thought God was saying to the church. This might take the form of a verse, words from a song, or a statement. During music at the conclusion of the sermon, they brought their notes up front and posted them on bulletin boards. "They came up with some pretty profound themes,"[36] Stephanie says. These were all typed up and brought back to the congregation.

Mill City Church has four worship teams. "Our number one goal," Stephanie emphasizes, "is to have people participate. We tell our teams, 'Participation is the new excellence.' Sometimes the music from the teams is so good people just listen instead of singing."[37] To prevent that, each team has two leaders. The band leader focuses on the musicians (repeating a verse or adding a chorus). The congregational leader focuses on the congregation to make certain people are connecting and singing. He or she is the one who speaks between songs, helping people get spiritually attuned for the next song. "A typical worship leader tries to play both roles," Stephanie observes. "However, it's difficult to lead musicians and help encourage participation by the congregation at the same time and do it well."[38]

When Mill City people take part in mission trips, they are asked to come up front to share the vision and what they will be doing. A couple from the church with degrees in environmental science have been in Ghana for a year-and-a-half working on a water project. They have supplied video updates, which are shown

---

[36] Ibid.
[37] Ibid.
[38] Ibid.

during the Sunday meeting. And when they return, they will report back to the congregation.

Neighborhood Alliance Church *(now Sojourn)*, Lacey, WA
| Greeting | **Encouraging** | **Spurring On** | Teaching/Instructing |
| **Serving** | Praying For | Confessing |

This account comes from my own experience in a church we planted in 1986. I served eight years as the bivocational pastor, then another 13 as senior pastor on the full-time church payroll.

Right from the time we launched the church, we observed the Lord's Supper once a month as many churches do—with mini cubes of bread and silver trays full of tiny cups that hold about a half ounce. After our first communion celebration, a man I had met just a few weeks before came up and thanked me profusely for our thoughtfulness for including empty cups in the serving trays. My puzzled look probably communicated more than I intended, so he explained: "I am an alcoholic, and I was able to participate by taking a cup without drinking anything." Marveling at his openness, I clarified: "We use grape juice, not wine, in the cups. The reason for the empties is that, still being a brand new church, we have more cups than people."

As the years passed, we filled more and more of the cups—and even purchased additional trays. But the more I studied the practices of the early church, the less satisfied I became with the way we were doing Communion. So, with the blessing of the elders, we began experimenting with making the "supper" part of the event into a real meal—a contemporary version of the first Lord's Supper in that upper room.

We had purposely constructed our building with a multipurpose room as our main meeting space. So on the first Sunday of each month, we filled the room with rectangular folding tables. Between each table and the next we placed two rows of chairs. During the first part of the meeting, which included singing and the sermon, all the chairs were turned to face the front. After that, half the chairs were turned around 180 degrees, so that people faced each other during the meal, thus making conversation both easy and natural.

By then the church had a number of cell groups, and each one took its turn at preparing the meal. We emphasized the need to keep the menu simple—often soup, bread, and perhaps a salad. The families of the cell group providing the meal did the serving, including the children and young people.

Each month the message for Communion Sunday focused on some aspect of Jesus's death and its meaning for us. Then, during the meal, we paused as we shared the bread and later the cup, during which times someone briefly helped us focus on the significance of each. Conversations across the tables liberated us from any somber stiffness, yet the focus on the meaning of the bread and cup preserved the seriousness of what we were remembering. We found that dining together restored a sense of family and one-anothering. On each table we included a few suggested conversation-starters designed to stimulate mutual encouragement and spurring on.

The transition included a learning curve. Since we were crossing over into what for us was uncharted territory, we had to learn from our successes and failures. One older couple, long-time church people, initially chose not to come to first-Sunday-of-the-month meetings. They had never seen Communion celebrated that way before. But after a few months, hearing good reports from others, they returned and eventually became staunch advocates of the "new" way of doing things.

Network Church, St. Albans, UK

| Greeting | **Encouraging** | **Spurring On** | **Teaching/Instructing** |
| **Serving** | **Praying For** | Confessing |

The term *servant leadership* is more than a mere catchphrase in this church. The leaders have deliberately laid aside their prerogatives in order to make room for others to exercise their ministry gifts. As a result, those in this congregation are able, even in their Sunday meetings, to serve one another in love. The following is based on an interview with church leader Trevor Withers.

Transitioning to a one-anothering format in its Sunday gatherings posed fewer difficulties for Network than for many other churches. Having been planted as a cell church where the small groups are highly participatory "put us ahead of the curve a bit,"[39] says Withers. Even so this congregation had to find its own

---

[39] Trevor Withers, interview by author, October 15, 2015.

rhythms and patterns. According to their website, a key value is "Holding deep convictions but being unfazed by questions."[40]

In the early days, to help embed this kind of openness into the DNA of the church, Withers invited "Rachel," an unbeliever, to visit their weekly gathering and state up front her questions about the Christian life. Some of those in the church thought Withers had gone way too far this time. Others welcomed the opportunity to hear her.

Rachel had often come for the Sunday lunches but only rarely for Network services. She had grown up in a home in which both parents were atheists, and had begun serious questioning when she was in her late teen years. "I am clearly seeking something," she told the congregation, "but I am not finding it." Her first question had to do with human sinfulness. Why would an all-powerful, holy God, she wondered, need a relationship with us if we are sinful? The session with Rachel lasted more than half an hour, with good-natured dialogue between her and several in the congregation.

The three-person leadership team deliberately created what they call a leadership vacuum. "Whatever we do," Withers says, "others cannot do, because we are taking up and occupying that space."[41] So the team set about equipping others to step into ministry roles. Today, their preaching team numbers around 18 and they have eight worship leaders. A number of people serve as

---

[40] "Our Network Distinctives," Network Church, accessed April 11, 2016, http://www.networkchurch.org/Groups/248573/Network_Church/About_Us/Our_Distinctives/Our_Distinctives.aspx.

[41] Withers, interview.

hosts to lead the weekly gatherings. "We try to bring a small group atmosphere into the Sunday morning space,"[42] Withers says. Typically, a Sunday gathering numbers from 40 to 45 people, with nearly twice that many in cell groups that meet during the week.

The Sunday meeting, which normally runs about 90 minutes, is divided into thirds. The first 30 minutes or so of "sung worship" is highly participatory. Singing makes up the core of this segment. Occasionally those in the congregation suggest songs, but the music is more often chosen by those leading on that particular Sunday. The key here is an introductory explanation that helps people feel safe to contribute. Anyone, though, may break in at any time between songs. Some pray. Others read Scripture or offer words of encouragement or insight. Three doors, fastened side-by-side and covered with blank paper, provide an opportunity for children—as well as adults—to write or draw pictures. So this section combines a measure of predictability with a free flow.

The second 20- or 30-minute period is devoted to hearing from each other. "We try to avoid the Christianese term 'testimony,'"[43] says Withers. The meeting host will begin by asking something like, "How have you encountered God this week?" Or, to counteract the tendency to divide the sacred from the secular, "What's been happening?" The biggest challenge in leading this segment, Withers acknowledges, is "holding your nerve—waiting

---

[42] "Our Network Distinctives," Network Church, accessed April 11, 2016, http://www.networkchurch.org/Groups/248573/Network_Church/About_Us/Our_Distinctives/Our_Distinctives.aspx.

[43] Withers, interview.

for what can sometimes seem like forever for someone to share."[44]
He discourages the hosts from sharing their own experiences,
urging them to put up with the pain of waiting. "The more we have
done this, the more people are coming prepared to share,"[45]
Withers says.

On some Sundays during this second section leaders will
engage in conversations with each other up front. This
demonstrates that the church leaders are communicating with
each other and tacitly gives permission for others to share as well.
Questions are encouraged. Prayer requests welcomed. Prayer can
take various forms—sometimes an individual praying with the
person who asked for it. For major concerns, the host may ask
everyone to stand, extend hands, and pray. At other times, the
congregation breaks into small groups to pray.

Formal teaching takes place in the final half hour. At the
time of my interview with Withers, the teaching/preaching team
was beginning a series of expositional messages through
Colossians. This will probably continue for a number of months.
Members of this team rotate. It is unusual for the same person to
preach two Sundays in a row, unless dealing with a particular
passage that were to require it. The teaching section often
concludes with a Q & A time, prompted by questions such as,
"What did you learn this morning?" or "What are you thinking?"

Once each month the Network gathering is an "All-
Together Sunday," in which the children remain with the adults

---

[44] Ibid.
[45] Ibid.

throughout the entire meeting. The emphasis here is on dramatizing Bible stories. "We need to retell the stories," Withers says, "to counteract the biblical illiteracy so prevalent in this post-Christendom era."[46] A team of five or six people work together to plan how to shape the presentation of each month's story, aiming to get the congregation to interact with it. According to Withers, "This takes us out of our heads and into our bodies."[47]

After observing how Network Church functions, a local Methodist pastor told Withers he was surprised at the kind of participation taking place. "This happens because you have exceptional people," he said. Withers disagrees: "We have these people because this is what we do."[48] Some have said none of this would be possible in a larger group. But Withers disagrees. "There should be ways of making this happen even in larger groups."[49]

New Day Church, Tacoma, WA

| **Greeting** | **Encouraging** | Spurring On | **Teaching/Instructing** |
| Serving | Praying For | Confessing |

By choice, the New Day congregation of approximately 300 still meets in the cafeteria of Meeker Middle School. Their website says: "From the start, our goal has been to strip away the baggage that sometimes goes along with church -- the trappings that get in the way of pursuing God. We wanted to create a warm, caring

---

[46] Ibid.
[47] Ibid.
[48] Ibid.
[49] Ibid.

community where people can come with their pain and their questions."[50] Jeff Peabody (yes, he is our son) planted the church in 2003. In the following account he describes some of the ways New Day incorporates participation on Sunday mornings.

In the fall of 2015 I did a preaching series out of the book of Joshua, calling it "A Bold Season." To the degree possible, we wanted to make the series interactive. On the music side we introduced and taught everyone a song written by three members of the congregation. Because this song was used throughout the series, the church body learned it well and it became their own theme song.

For several weeks, following the sermon, everyone received a take-home card. It included a key verse as well as a couple of questions to prompt people to watch for certain things in their life experiences. For example, one of the cards suggested that they be on the lookout for a time when God gave them courage during the week. The next Sunday we revisited that theme, giving opportunity for people to share. Some told of times they had seen God give them courage. Others related how they had faced a situation in which they lacked courage and asked God to supply them with it.

During these weeks we also tied the greeting time to the theme. As we gathered, I suggested a series-related question for use in welcoming others. The question needed to be as non-threatening as possible and one everyone could respond to. For example, one question was: "What's one thing you miss from the 80s? If you weren't alive then, find someone who was and ask about something you THINK was true in the 80s." While not

---

[50] "Welcome," New Day Church, accessed April 13, 2016, http://www.newdaynw.com/about/welcome/.

requiring much spiritual depth, the question did generate involvement. As the message began, I revisited the question, collected a few answers from the congregation, then launched into my own response that connected it with the sermon. This has proved to be a good tool for generating good conversation during the greeting time and creating a collective experience that provides continuity throughout the rest of the service.

A couple of times during the Joshua series, I knew about a story in someone's life that related to what I planned to teach. So I asked that person to come up and share it as an illustration right during the sermon. In other cases, those who were facing difficult, long-term life situations actually gave the whole message on the courage-related theme.

Our series culminated Thanksgiving week. That Sunday—as we do each year during that week—we divided the congregation into breakout groups. Each group received a ring that held cards on which were printed a recap of key verses, themes, and points covered during the series. Those in the group were to tell which they most identified with and why. As in other years, some people, uncomfortable in breakout groups, avoided coming that Sunday. To alleviate that discomfort, I try to make certain each group includes a volunteer facilitator who can guide the discussion and lead in prayer.

My goal is to have someone from the congregation preach once a month, without pulling in a guest speaker from the outside. We now have probably a dozen or so who are willing and able to do this. So I can now go a full year without having to ask anyone to repeat—unless they have a series in mind. I seek to communicate that preaching is a team ministry, making it clear that when others preach they are not simply subbing for me. This takes time, because I walk each speaker through sermon preparation with coaching, guidance, and support. I'm trying to follow the example of a seminary professor who once said, "I'm always working myself out of a job." Even so, there is always plenty to do.[51]

Northwood Church, Maple Grove, MN

| Greeting | **Encouraging** | **Spurring On** | Teaching/Instructing |
| Serving | Praying For | **Confessing** |

Almost every Sunday Northwood Church includes what they call "FaithStories" in their main gathering. Typically running about five minutes, each is a personal testimony spoken by someone from the congregation. Here is the transcript of a recent FaithStory given by Rachel Bichler.

Have you ever had a sneaking suspicion that you just weren't good enough? That no matter how hard you try, you just don't have what it takes? I know I have. It's something that has haunted me for my entire life. For as long as I can remember, I have struggled with the idea that I'm somehow lacking. As a child I felt awkward, unable to connect with my peers. I was sure I could never be as relaxed and confident as the other kids appeared to be. At home, even though I was always quite sure that my parents loved me, I never felt quite sure that I deserved it.

Those very same misgivings also applied to my relationship with Christ. I became a Christian at a very young age. I'm not even sure just how old I was; only that it was a long

---

[51] Jeff Peabody, interview by author, December 26, 2015.

time ago, in a Sunday school classroom, joined in prayer by a teacher whose name I no longer remember.

I was very lucky in that way, to be raised from infancy in a Christian home. My parents were also regular church attendees. Some of my earliest memories are of time spent in Sunday school. As I got older, I became active in youth group, went to Christian summer camps, and participated in missions work. I got to know other Christian kids my own age and made some good friends.

And yet, the older I got the more I felt like a fraud. I couldn't escape from my continuing sense of inadequacy. I was certain that I was not as good a person as those around me. If they only knew my secret thoughts and secret sins I was sure they would recoil in horror. I often wondered how Jesus could love me when I couldn't even love myself.

Then, in my teenage years, I began to surround myself with people that didn't make me feel so inferior. I found people who had no place for morals or judgment. My new friends drank alcohol, did drugs, partied, lied, stole, and slept around. Eager for acceptance, I joined in their lifestyle with hardly a backward glance.

And although I continued to think of myself as a Christian, I avoided attending church. I couldn't help comparing myself to the others there and thinking they would all look down on me. After all, I wasn't living a Christian lifestyle.

My season of disobedience, self-loathing, and perpetual running from God lasted for more than 10 years. At the end I found myself divorced, and living back at home with my parents, and feeling utterly lost.

It was then, at a time when I was more broken than I had ever been, that I began to turn to God for healing. You see, even though I had spent many years running from him and his

166

judgment, he was never far away. In fact, throughout my long rebellion, he never once gave up on me. He was just waiting for me to be broken enough to realize my need for him.

My return to faith wasn't easy. It didn't go perfectly. I struggled and backslid more than once. The biggest hurdle of all was my shame. I knew that God offered perfect love and forgiveness through Jesus Christ, but I had a very hard time accepting it. More than ever I knew that I could never be good enough.

But, with a will surely strengthened by God, this time I didn't give up. I read my Bible. I started attending church more regularly. I practiced confessing my sins and asking God's forgiveness. Slowly but surely I began to feel the presence of Jesus in my life.

Then I met my future husband, Matt, a seeker like myself, and things began to snowball. I could feel the hand of God gently pushing us together. We began attending Northwood together and in it found a welcoming place where we could grow in our rediscovered faith. When we were married a year later, we committed ourselves to regular church attendance and raising our children to know and love Jesus.

Since that time, my faith has continued to grow. Every day I come to rely a little more on the power of God's sustaining love. As for my feelings of inadequacy, the truth is I still struggle. The difference is that I no longer have to struggle alone. I know now that I can take my weakness to Jesus and that he will use it to make me strong. I know that even though I will never be good enough in this life, God will still love me and forgive me and continue his work in me as long as my heart remains open to him.[52]

How many Christians, like Rachel, struggle with the haunting thought that they are not good enough? Imagine the encouragement of hearing a fellow member from their own church body admit to this and describe her journey as she learned how to deal with it through faith. This is one-anothering.

Telling her story to the church in its main weekly gathering required Rachel to lay down her life for others in that congregation. First, it required hours of prayer, thought, meeting with a coach, writing, and rewriting several drafts. Second, it meant being transparent and vulnerable.

Stories of this quality are not unusual at Northwood, because those who tell them are equipped to do so by one of the pastors. Brian Doten says preparation for each story often begins months ahead of time. Normally, each story passes through three or four revisions before it reaches the final draft.

The time and effort invested in the development of these testimonies pay off not only in the lives of those who hear on a given Sunday. Those who have been coached through the preparation process often find that they are now prepared to tell their FaithStories to coworkers, neighbors, relatives, and others long after the initial presentation to the church family.

---

[52] Rachel Bichler, "Rachel's FaithStory," March 31, 2013, Northwood Church, audio recording, accessed April 12, 2016, http://northwood.cc/2013/04/11/rachels-faithstory-4-7-2013/. Reprinted with permission.

If the demographics in your church run parallel to those for the United States, approximately half the congregation is in the labor force. Those employed full-time may easily put in nearly 100,000 hours over a lifetime. In other words, they are investing the bulk of their prime-time waking hours in the workplace. That is where their faith will be lived out for better or for worse. And in today's work world, Christians need frequent spurring on to maintain the good works to which God has called them in Christ. In another Northwood Church FaithStory, Brandon Kohler told about how a sermon had encouraged him "to actively reflect God's love and compassion in everyday life, more specifically in the workplace."[53] Here is an excerpt from the transcript of what he shared with the congregation:

> Over the years, the mention of faith in the workplace has become more of a whisper and in lots of places a total silence as it's against company policy. This is where I felt God was calling me to make a difference. . . .
>
> In my job I have the opportunity to interact with so many people in a given day. I manage 18 technicians in the field and work closely with 25 others in the office. As a leader in the company I have a lot of eyes on me. It's important that I am a good example and practice the core values of my company. But I realized that all those people are seeing much more than just how I represent the company. They see who I am as they watch my reactions and how I handle situations with others. Northwood Church helped me find a place for God in that leadership role. You've helped encourage me to bring God up in

---

[53] Brandon Kohler, e-mail message to author, September 8, 2015.

discussions, give glory to God when sharing accomplishments with my employees, and challenge others to reflect Christ throughout the day in their customers' homes.

God has provided me many tools at work to do just this, but it's not easy as I am sure you can all understand. As I reached a point where I wanted to connect on a deeper level with some of my coworkers, I struggled to find the time and place to do that during work hours. God did not hesitate to bring my mind back to an idea he provided me about a year ago. On April 29 at 4:29 p.m. in 2014 at my desk, God struck me with an idea. At the time it seemed random, which is I am sure why it slowly lost its legs, but here I find out he was preparing me for this challenge.

That idea was "Office Change." Throughout the month, coworkers will take their change they find in their desk or in their car and drop it into the Office Change jar. Then at the end of the month we will take a trip to Feed My Starving Children, donate the change, and make a difference for starving children. I feel God pulling on my heart to make a difference, and thanks to Northwood I have been able to connect with God again and will continue to carry out his plan for me as it comes.[54]

(The written guidelines given to those who will present their FaithStories in Northwood Church are included as Appendix A.)

---

[54] Ibid.

Peniel Wesleyan Tabernacle, Greater Georgetown, Guyana

| Greeting | Encouraging | Spurring On | Teaching/Instructing |
| Serving | **Praying For** | Confessing |

In many churches, the only prayer during the main congregational meeting is offered by the pastor in what has traditionally been called the pastoral prayer. But in the weekly gatherings of this church on the North Atlantic shore of South America, prayer (singular) has become prayers (plural).

The time set aside for praying for one another in this church of about 75 began when in 2011 it struck Michael Suffrienin, pastor, that he could not be there to pray for everyone. He knew the church body included many struggling and immature believers. But he also knew of many stronger Christians who could influence and help them.

So one Sunday, during the worship service, he simply asked for a pause in which he shared a brief Bible passage relating to prayer. Then, after identifying a particular issue the church was facing at that time, he asked people to find a partner and join together in prayer for that concern.

When the church had grown accustomed to partnering in prayer during their main weekly gathering, he expanded the scope of prayer subjects by asking anyone with a need for prayer to share that with someone else and then pray for each other. These sessions of one-another prayer have included such concerns as family challenges, financial worries, loss of loved ones, and recovery after theft or flood damage. Although this prayer time is not a part of every meeting, when included it typically takes 10 to 15 minutes.

No one has raised any objections to this practice. However, some who are new or uncomfortable praying with others tend to remain in their seats during this time.[55]

Salvation Army Berry Street Worship Center, Nashville, TN

| Greeting | Encouraging | Spurring On | **Teaching/Instructing** |
| Serving | Praying For | Confessing |

Steve Simms, core administrator for this Salvation Army church, posted this blog entitled, "Are Sermons Effective?"

Have you ever tested the effectiveness of sermons? I did.

I was a brand new pastor in my first church — Mayfield Cumberland Presbyterian Church in Mayfield, Kentucky. After finishing three years of seminary, I had been preaching for about 10 weeks to about 20 people each Sunday morning and evening.

The response to my sermons was less than overwhelming, so one Sunday afternoon I decided to test the effectiveness of my sermons. I thought of one simple and easy question about the main topic of each of my first 10 or so Sunday morning sermons. Then that Sunday night, rather than preaching, I gave an oral test and asked the congregation the questions.

---

[55] Vedawattie Ram, e-mail message to author, January 12, 2016.

How many people do you think got at least one of my questions right? None. Nobody could answer any of my simple questions — not even my question about my sermon from that very morning. I was shocked. No one could remember even the basic point of any of my sermons.

I continued to preach (that was my job description) but from that point on, I never thought my sermons could do much. A message prepared in a mind has little power, even in a church setting. To reach people requires more than facts, doctrines, and poems.

With all the preaching in our churches, American Christianity remains ineffective. It is captured by our culture and follows trends rather than creating them. Rather than influencing society toward more noble and virtuous lifestyles, American Christianity has been influenced into following society's fads.

Perhaps something more than sermons is needed. According to Paul of Tarsus, a church meeting should be built around open participation. He wrote: "When you come together everyone has a hymn, or a word of instruction, a revelation, a tongue or an interpretation." This is a much more effective way to help people change than a lecture each week by a professional.

When Alcoholics Anonymous (AA) was started they considered how to hold their meetings. They decided to build their meetings around open participation rather than using the weekly lecture format. Their membership exploded and they quickly became one of the most effective groups in treating alcoholics.

When people passively sit and listen, little happens, however, when they openly participate they grow. An old saying puts it this way: "Christianity is better caught than taught." Perhaps the church should try Paul's instructions."[56]

Sampa Community Church, Sao Paulo, Brazil

| Greeting | Encouraging | Spurring On | Teaching/Instructing |

| Serving | Praying For | Confessing |

Sampa (short for Sao Paulo) Community Church began in the home of Pete and Jane Hawkins. From about ten people initially, the church eventually grew to around 120. Because Pete worked full time for Rolls-Royce in another Brazilian city, Jane handled the lion's share of the startup effort. With no teaching pastor, right from the beginning the church viewed and listened to DVDs of sermons by Andy Stanley, pastor of North Point Community Church in Atlanta, GA. During an interview Jane Hawkins told how they incorporated discussions into each week's congregational meeting in this bilingual church.

Describe the way the discussion times worked in Sampa Community Church.

Each week we projected on a screen up front an Andy Stanley message from a DVD series that included subtitles. After the people watched and listened to the 35-40 minute sermon, we

---

56 Steve Simms, "Are Sermons Effective?," *Free Gas For Your Think Tank (A blog to jog your mind and unclog your heart ...)* (blog), December 9, 2011, accessed April 12, 2016, https://stevesimms.wordpress.com/2011/12/09/are-sermons-effective/. Copyright Steve Simms. Used with permission.

divided them into discussion groups of about six, some for Portuguese and some for English speakers. If extras made a group larger, the leader encouraged them to find their way to other groups. We found that when groups went over six, quieter people didn't share or the talkative ones tended to dominate. Visitors were always assured in the initial announcement, "You are welcome to speak, but feel free just to listen if you prefer." Otherwise visitors could opt out and leave for fear of being put on the spot.

After the recorded sermon, we projected three questions on the screen all at once to facilitate dialogue in each of the groups. Each question related to the message, but we tried to word the first one in such a way that no one, including unbelievers, would feel excluded or threatened. For example, if the message had been on marriage, the first question might have been, "Tell us about the happiest marriage you know. What made it special?" The second went a little deeper, but kept a generic focus, avoiding "you." The third question was more intimate and applicational. By that time the stronger Christians or personalities were comfortable enough to share a little more deeply and led the way.

We always strictly limited the conversations to 15 minutes. A countdown timer in the corner of the screen helped to relax people and showed them 15 meant 15. Because they saw all three questions at once, it helped them think ahead about their responses. At the 15-minute mark the questions came down, replaced with "See You Next Week!" and soft music, so that people could finish their answers and/or close in prayer.

Why did you include the discussion time after each message?

For several reasons. First, ending the service just after the message seemed to us a poor stewardship of rich resources.

The congregation would hear Stanley's life-changing, profound, deep, and thought-provoking message, then the mood would be broken by either an upbeat song or dismissal. Out in the lobby conversation would center on the kids, the game, the weather—or worse, mere trivia.

Second, because we had a virtual pastor, we wanted to add more human warmth. This also helped us sell the idea of discussion groups. Right after Stanley said amen, we told the congregation, "Since our messages are on DVD, we want to add some human interaction by letting you get into groups and talk about what you just heard." We also said, "You usually don't get a platform to take issue with the pastor, but we're giving you a chance to do that today. Do you agree or disagree with what he said about . . . ? We're going to put three questions on the screen and let you talk about them for 15 minutes. After that you are all invited to have a cup of coffee in the lobby."

Third, our messages had originally been preached in Atlanta—and we were in Sao Paulo, Brazil—so the invitation to discuss it was appealing. "Talk about this message from Atlanta. Does it relate to life in Sao Paulo?" Of course it did, but the challenge got people's attention and engagement.

Fourth, we wanted the messages to change lives because we believe in transformation, not just information. We asked people practical application questions. A big part of remembering what you hear is talking about it and processing it out loud. If you can do that right away—hear the message and talk it over—it serves two purposes. Visitors and unbelievers are invited to push back if they wish. And Christians can say, I want to try doing that in my own life. It is rare for unbelievers to be encouraged to voice doubts and concerns in a church setting. And vocalizing an intention is a small step toward accountability for the Christians. Both groups take the content of the message a step deeper into their lives.

Fifth, not everybody participated in a small group during the rest of the week. Our discussions gave people a taste of sharing and listening to others that would hopefully draw them to join a community group. Meanwhile, they had a bit of the experience without having to commit or drive in Sao Paulo traffic.

Finally, visitors got close to people their first Sunday. Right away they would meet and hear personal stories from five strangers. So the next Sunday they had openings for conversation, as well as an emotional connection to a friendly face.

How did you prepare the discussion group facilitators?

The logistics of bivocational volunteers in a city of 20 million prevented us from providing an ideal amount of training. Basically, we looked for mature believers who were willing to lead, people who were socially sensitive and considerate of the feelings of unbelievers. In spite of the minimal training, the facilitators were given some guidelines:

- Do not call on people. Ever.
- Be comfortable with some silence while people think. Don't jump in with answers. Since you are seen as the authority, people will feel shut down if you come across as too spiritual.
- Do not allow criticism of other faiths or politics to stand. But be gracious.
- Remember the unbelievers in the group. Set the stage by being honest and vulnerable. Don't present yourself as a spiritual giant who reads your Bible every day or never has questions.

- Go first with a response to the third question—the harder, more personal question. Be honest. Be a struggler. Be real. And speak as little as possible so others can share their stories.

- Do not correct theology unless it is life or death. Keep the sharing about experiences, not theology.

Was your seating arrangement conducive to breaking into discussion groups?

The ideal, of course, is movable chairs, but over the ten years we were involved, the church met in various buildings. One had fixed chairs, another had pew-like benches. Even that worked, though, as we just asked people to turn around—and they managed to do it. This was also a reason for limiting the groups to six. If people are sitting on benches or pews, the smaller the group the easier it is to hear.

How have the discussion groups made a difference in the life of the congregation and the lives of individuals?

Let me give an example. Our children attended an international high school—very much a liberal, secularist place. Our son had a non-Christian teacher, Jason, who was about 29 years old. He represented exactly the kind of person we were trying to reach. So I approached him with a question: Would he be willing to visit our church and provide feedback from the viewpoint of a person who doesn't attend church? He agreed and came. Our first message series from Stanley was called *The Matrix*, and it was radically different from traditional church, with professional actors setting up the message and many references to the movie. I was sure this plus Stanley's compelling communication style would stand out to Jason. But when I asked him for his comments afterward about what he liked best, he skipped over Stanley's message, the movie theme, and the actors and said it was our discussion groups. He had felt totally free to disagree, to argue, to hold different opinions, and to say what he thought.

Circumstances required you to leave Sampa. Since then, the church has hired a teaching pastor from Dallas, TX. Yet the congregation has chosen to continue the discussion groups. Why?

Yes, the core group of church leaders decided to keep the discussion groups going. They had seen the power of these times to create community and to involve visitors. Discussion groups are a unique and engaging feature of Sampa. Instead of putting the questions on the screen, the new pastor writes questions and hands them out on paper. I think every church should have discussion groups. If pastors would adopt this practice, it would multiply the effects of their messages. Once people are engaged, they can immediately talk it over, argue, disagree, confirm, and affirm. This all leads to life transformation along a spiritual journey. I believe that should be the goal in every church, in every service, for every attender.[57]

Sumas Advent Christian Church, Sumas, WA

| Greeting | Encouraging | Spurring On | Teaching/Instructing |

| **Serving** | Praying For | Confessing |

Church potlucks have been the butt of countless one-liners. For example, someone said the only thing that ever changes is the color of the Jell-O® served at those dinners. But several years ago,

---

[57] Jane Hawkins, interview by author, January 4, 2016.

this pastor discovered how to make these meals participative in a whole new and healing way. The following account is based on an interview with Lowell Bakke.

In 2005, Lowell Bakke was asked to engage in an "intentional" interim pastorate in the Sumas Advent Christian Church to lead a renewal process in this more than century old congregation. This church had been in the center of the Sumas, WA community, with over ten percent of the community participating in the church for over a hundred years. However, in the five years previous to Bakke's involvement, the church had four different pastors, which was an indication that the congregation was in the middle of its worst ever discord in its 112-year history. Organizational, pastoral, and interpersonal conflicts had built high fences between people who had previously enjoyed close ties and significant community ministry for decades. The one thing they could agree on was the continuation of their monthly potluck dinners that had been part of the church's history as long as anyone could remember. But even those meals had become a challenge because of the discord in the church body.

Bakke noticed that when they came together for one of these dinners, they were still open enough to remark on what each other's best dish was. So he decided to help them apply to their Sunday dinners some of the appreciative inquiry principles they were already practicing . "You know one another's best potluck recipe," he told them. "So as we do more of these dinners, I'd like you to bring only your best dish. Then, during the meal, we'll ask you to explain why it is your best."[58] As relationships began to thaw, after hearing someone tell what they considered their best dish, someone else would chime in with, "No—that's not your best. I know that your best is really . . . ."

Although it technically came after, the meal was really an extension of the main Sunday gathering. Once they had become accustomed to focusing on their best menu items, Bakke challenged them to broaden the dialog into the Sunday morning church meeting. There, though, he encouraged them to describe how they remembered the church when they were at their best. "Do we want to be at our best again—and let go of when we were at our worst?"[59] he asked. So, in front of the entire congregation, they began to share stories of when the church was at its best. Conflicts ended, attendance improved, and the church is thriving today.

---

[58] Lowell Bakke, interview by author, August 23, 2016.
[59] Ibid.

Temple Baptist Church, Rockford, IL

| Greeting | Encouraging | Spurring On | **Teaching/Instructing** |
| Serving | Praying For | Confessing |

In just about any church, we can safely assume that the Holy Spirit has given teaching gifts to a few believers. For church leaders, this creates at least two questions: (a) How can those gifts be drawn out and developed? And (b) How can such people be given opportunities to use their gifts? Here is how one pastor met these challenges. The following is based on an interview with Lowell Bakke.

Several years ago, Gordon Hanstad was serving as pastor of Temple Baptist Church in Rockford, IL. Then in my twenties, I served on his staff. Pastor Hanstad said he recognized in me a gift of being able to link Scripture to the everyday lives of Christians. "You're not a researcher," he told me. "You're not a Hebrew or Greek scholar. But no one applies Scripture better than you do." He then offered to teach me how to preach in four weeks. "Are you serious?" I asked. "In just four weeks?"

On each of the next four Friday afternoons, Pastor Hanstad provided me with a draft of the sermon he had written for that week. It included all the biblical research and text explanations. But it was missing any application. "Okay," he said, "for the next four Sundays you and I will share the pulpit. After I speak, you will have seven minutes on Sunday morning to apply this message to our congregation." Although he had no clue what I might say, he followed through on this arrangement. The jointly presented messages were even broadcast on radio.

Shortly afterward, when I began to serve as a pastor, I found five or six trusted pastors and writers as well as gifted teachers within the small congregation whose scholarship and research I could trust as a foundation for my messages. These people did not come from the same theological position, which made the sermons more kingdom thinking rather than a denominational or systematic theology approach to preaching. I then created a message of application from what they had produced. Through this practice, in both churches that I served as lead pastor, gifts were recognized and developed. And the meetings for the main congregation became more participatory.[60]

The Church on the Way, Van Nuys, CA

| Greeting | Encouraging | Spurring On | Teaching/Instructing |
| Serving | **Praying For** | Confessing |

Shortly after Jack Hayford retired from his pastoring role, Ollie Malone, then a student at the King's Seminary, decided to attend The Church on the Way while taking classes in Van Nuys. Here is how he remembers the first Sunday meeting he attended:

> I was surprised when Pastor Jack (who, although retired, was leading the service that morning, but not preaching) asked the congregation to form in groups of four or so members, introduce ourselves, and identify any specific prayer needs we might have. I ended up in a group with three other men who were alone at the time. Quickly we shared names and prayer needs, then took to the task of prayer.

---

[60] Lowell Bakke, interview by author, August 13, 2015.

To this day (more than ten years later), I recall the prayer needs shared with me: one young Indian father shared the challenges that he and his wife were having with a four-year-old daughter, another young brother asked for prayer for his mother who did not know Christ, the third asked for prayer for a mother who was ill. I needed to have my house in Houston sold, since I had moved away and it had not been sold. We prayed for each other's needs and returned to our seats.

In each of the services that I attended, the practice was reinforced. I prayed for and got to know several individuals during the course of my days there. Throughout the days that followed, I would continue to attend services that would occur during the week. Frequently, I would see one of the three men with whom I had prayed on that first Sunday morning. We would ask for updates on the prayer needs. "How are things going with your daughter?" I recall asking my Indian brother. I was blessed to hear, "So much better."

I have often thought how simple the request was at The Church on the Way, yet how powerful and transformative it was in my life and, I suspect, in the lives of others who still believe in praying for one another, as the Scripture exhorts.[61]

---

[61] Ollie Malone, e-mail message to author, July 25, 2015.

The Evergreen Community, Portland, OR

| Greeting | Encouraging | Spurring On | **Teaching/Instructing** |
| Serving | Praying For | Confessing |

In this church the Sunday congregation numbers approximately 100. Planted by Bob Hyatt, who still serves as one of the pastors/elders, the church meets in an open warehouse space. Hyatt, a graduate of Western Seminary, was interviewed by *Christianity Today*'s PreachingToday.com in 2008, which published a three-part conversation on dialogical preaching. In the introduction to that series, the editor wrote: "Under the conviction that the audience doesn't have to be silent, some preachers are embracing dialogical preaching."[62] Wanting to learn more, I interviewed Hyatt in his Portland office.

What led to your decision to move to dialogical preaching?
A couple of things. First, back in 2000 people were asking, "If we had to start a church from the ground up, what would it look like today?" As I thought about that, I saw that meetings in the early church involved a discussion of the apostles' teachings. This, I thought, should be a part of our practice today, which meant that a 40-minute lecture might not be the best way. Looking back to my seminary classes, I knew that my favorites involved interaction. So I naturally asked myself: What if I were to ask questions—as preachers do and are

---

[62] "Dialogical Preaching (Part 1)," Preaching Today, accessed April 13, 2016, http://www.preachingtoday.com/skills/themes/energyofsynergy/dialogicalpreaching1.html.

encouraged to do—but actually to wait for people to answer them? My homiletics and preaching classes had emphasized that questions are valuable tools, but they were always meant to be rhetorical questions. To me, this felt as if we were shortchanging people.

Second—and this was a huge theological shift for me—I came to realize that, although I am the recognized preacher, I might not have the most important thing to say on a given Sunday morning. That insight worked a bit of humility into me as a pastor and communicator. I am not Moses coming down off the mountain. Instead, I am leading a community and facilitating our learning from the inspired Word of God. The inspiration is not coming from my mouth but from the biblical page and the Spirit working in our community. Yes, I have a fairly central role in that on a Sunday morning, but what I say may not end up being the most important thing. I've noticed that when someone other than the preacher begins to speak in a congregational gathering, people sit up and lean forward. This is valuable, because it signals engagement.

What are some of the most important lessons you've learned since you began preaching dialogically?

Number one, it's a skill that you need to engage with and intentionally aim to improve. The first component of this skill is learning how to ask the right kind of questions. When I first started preaching this way, my questions tended to be closed-ended. I leaned more toward questions in the Bible knowledge category. While these have some value, they tend to make non-Christians and new Christians feel dumb. Such questions are less helpful than those that draw out where people are and what they are experiencing.

This Sunday we'll be starting through the book of Colossians and I'll be dealing with how God brought Paul out of the kingdom of darkness into the kingdom of light. I do plan to ask a question that involves Bible knowledge, but I'll ask it in a way that will be helpful to those who don't know the story. I'll say, "For those of us who don't know the story of Paul, can someone fill us in?" Yes, it is a "Bible-knowledge-ish" sort of question, but it will come across in a way that those unaware of Paul's story will find helpful rather than confusing or patronizing. I could very quickly and succinctly tell the story of Paul's conversion on the road to Damascus. But if the community can do it just as well as I can, and if people tend to lean forward when one of their peers is speaking, why wouldn't I let them do that?

The second component of learning this skill involves body language. I've found that through my body language I can help people know when to start and to stop talking. Sometimes people are reticent. They just sit there. This may be because I have not done a good job of getting the congregation warmed up. But if I demonstrate a real openness in my facial expression, as well as in what I say, it can draw people out. At other times some people will speak on and on and I've had to learn how to shut them down. One way is to jump in when they take a breath and simply reflect back what they have said. "So what I hear you saying is 'X, Y, and Z.' Thank you—and now who else?" Or by turning slightly, my body language will help to focus attention in another direction. We have had people who like to hear their own voices, but this is far less a problem than it was in our early days.

Another lesson I've learned in preaching dialogically is that it takes time to develop the skill. Give yourself as much grace as you would anyone else. This is not something they teach in homiletics classes. Be prepared for mornings when it does not work well. But I learned something about dialogical preaching even on those mornings that were somewhat painful.

Finally, I learned how effective silences can be in a dialogical preaching situation. Because we preachers have learned the art of speaking, we have a tendency to want to fill in the gaps. If I receive no response after asking a noncritical question, I may say something like, "Okay, I did not craft that question well. Let's move on." But if I'm asking a question vital in the formation of the people—and no one says anything—we will just sit there. I'll let people think about it. I may take a sip of coffee, look at my notes, or look at the congregation. Really interesting and important things happen during those minutes, and I think people would be shortchanged if I answered for them. Sometimes it just takes the patience to throw something out there and let it simmer, to let people even become uncomfortable with the silence. Because it is in that space that they are being forced to do some internal work: "Why is this question making me uncomfortable? I really wish I didn't have to think about this, but I guess I do."

How does the dialogical message typically unfold on a Sunday?

The sermons are in three parts. In part one, the introduction, I ask open-ended questions to help orient the congregation to where we are going with the message. For example, this Sunday, in the message about the Saul–Paul transformation, I plan to ask: "Thinking back on your life over the past couple of years, what is a change in your life that you would never have imagined ten years ago?" I might ask a couple of these introductory questions to help people get comfortable with the idea of change in the lives of people. After the dialogue resulting from the questions, we go into the passage of Scripture for that morning.

In part two, we explore the Scripture passage together. The goal: to get the community to engage with the text. Here, I still ask questions, but they are less open-ended and more interpretive. I might say, "What do you think Paul is getting at in this passage?" I aim to be sensitive here, because the people have not spent the week in commentaries as I have. But in this section of the sermon, I give the congregation a chance to do some of the heavy lifting. They come up with a spectrum of answers. Most of the time, among those given, I will hear one that does a great job of describing the meaning of the text. But the beauty of it is that it is coming from them, not from me. I might say something like, "We can learn something from all these responses, but the one I want to zero in on is . . . ." This lets me emphasize the best response without making anyone feel like theirs was wrong. One time Dustin, a fellow pastor/elder, paused significantly after hearing the answer to one of his questions. Then he said, "You know, that's better than what I was going to say!"

Part three doesn't contain much dialogue. Here is where I cover what I have been praying over, studying, and thinking about all week. So in this final section of the sermon, I present the implications of the passage for our lives, explaining the challenges this text presents to us as individuals and as a community.

But the sermon is not the climax of the morning. After the dialogical message, we come to the Communion Table, sing, and respond to what we have heard. Each week I try to ask: "What have you heard God saying to you today? Once, after we had explored Isaiah 58, it came up that we are not to turn our backs on relatives in need. In our community was a busy, professional couple who had never had any children. The husband was a psychologist and the wife a lawyer. Her sister, addicted to drugs, had just had her children taken from her. This couple, in response to "What have you heard God saying to you today?" told the community: "We heard clearly that we need to take these kids." So they instantly went from zero to three children. The church, having heard them share God's call on their lives, pitched in and helped support them.

What advice might you have for those wanting to transition to dialogical preaching?

Take it slow. Prepare people for it. Sudden changes cause disequilibrium. When I was in seminary, I worked in a highly traditional church—a piano on one side, an organ on the other. After the pastor returned from an out-of-state conference, he moved in a single Sunday from piano and organ to drums and guitars. Half the congregation got up and walked out—and never came back.

If your people are not used to dialogical preaching, consider starting with just one question. Make it one that actually matters. It is easiest to begin with tell-us-something-about-yourself questions. If you're preaching on God being present in our lives, ask something like: "What is one time when you felt God really present in your life?" Let people tell you their stories, then in your sermon, refer back to what they said: "As Joe said earlier . . . "

What positive results have you observed as a result of dialogical preaching?

Visitors are immediately engaged. I'd estimate that about 25 percent of our visitors will say something on a Sunday morning. This way of preaching produces an active engagement that goes far beyond passive listening. Even the best of us will tune in and out while listening to a monological message. But when someone asks us a question that forces us internally to answer it—even if we don't speak our answer out loud—there is a level of connection that rises well above listening to a lecture. We value dialogical preaching so much that we have said we never want to get over a certain size. Instead, we'll plant churches and remain fraternally connected.[63]

Westview Bible Church, Pierrefonds, Quebec, Canada
| Greeting | **Encouraging** | Spurring On | **Teaching/Instructing** |
| **Serving** | Praying For | Confessing |

On their website, Westview Bible says, "We find discipleship happens in community through loving, vital, and meaningful relationships with others who are also growing in Christ-likeness."[64] They seek to nurture these relationships not only in small groups but also in a weekly meeting of the entire congregation. The following is based on an interview with Nita Kotiuga, who serves as Westview's pastor for care ministries and spiritual formation. She began by explaining how the church has started changing their Communion Services in ways that create opportunities for members of the congregation to serve one another.

On the first Sunday of each month we celebrate Communion. The elements are prayed over by people in the congregation. In the last six months I have concentrated on inviting our young adults to do this. They range from 17 to 24 years old. I choose from that particular age group because it is a

---

[63] Bob Hyatt, interview by author, October 22, 2015.
[64] "Group Life," Westview Bible Church, accessed April 13, 2016, http://www.westviewlife.org/group-life.

way of involving them. Older people have more access to the platform than these Millennials. We sometimes have the congregation file down to the front to receive the elements. On those Sundays, we involve people who may not have a public role to hold the elements.

In response to requests for spoken testimonies, we have begun asking two from the congregation to tell their stories during the Communion service. I usually ask people who are not in the limelight, seeking "average" believers that others can identify with. Some people have even come to me asking for a time to share their stories. When I introduce the speakers I try to mention something unique and beautiful about each one.

Normally we schedule baptisms on the same week as Communion. Ahead of time, those who will be baptized choose someone in the congregation to serve them by baptizing them—a fellow believer who has mentored them or been of significant spiritual help. This past week, we had three baptisms, which involved six people. I held the towels and briefed everyone. It was so much fun to see more people involved.[65]

If you were to visit Westview Bible Church on a typical Sunday morning, you might be surprised to see that the paid pastors do only the welcome and benediction. In this church of 550 attendees (Sunday attendance averaging about 375), most of the preaching/teaching is done by a "core preaching team" made up of five members of the congregation. (Three others, not on this central team, may preach once or twice a year.) Currently the core team includes a stay-at-home mom, a school teacher, a scientist, a

---

[65] Nita Kotiuga, interview by author, October 29, 2015.

self-employed businessman, and a dentist. On average, each of these speaks approximately once per month.

One of the paid pastors, Jeff Simunic oversees community development and outreach and is responsible for all the ministries of the church. Nita Kotiuga explained why Westview adopted this team approach, which stands in such a contrast to the preaching practice of most other congregations: "It is important that those in the congregation hear from those in the trenches, from their peers and not just from professionals." She added, "We see preaching as a gift. Not everyone in leadership necessarily has that gift."[66]

How does Westview Bible Church identify those with a preaching gift?

It varies. One person on the core preaching team came from another church that recommended him as highly capable in this area. The stay-at-home mom was asked to pray one Sunday, and the church leadership recognized her ability to connect with the congregation. The gifting of one of the elders was recognized through his leadership of Bible studies.

Each week, all members of the core team review the content that one of them will present the following Sunday. This provides a safeguard against erroneous teaching and adds depth to the material used for illustrations. The head of the preaching team is responsible for coaching in sermon development, use of PowerPoint, and so on. Training, though, is really a team effort. All of them carefully evaluate feedback from the congregation.

---

[66] Ibid.

Although Kotiuga sits in on meetings of the preaching team, she says, "I don't have time to preach."[67]

Her time, just as that of the other paid pastor, is devoted to preparing people in the church to do the work of ministry (Eph. 4:11, 12). "We jokingly tell people," she said, "that Westview Bible Church has a hundred pastors."[68] Those involved in any group related to the church, whether it be hockey, basketball, or line dancing, are responsible to care for others in that group. For example, when a new baby arrives in the family of someone in the group, the others reach out with meals and other forms of ministry. Doing church with such a high level of participation involves a tremendous amount of work, she says.

What has been the response of the congregation to having the preaching done by non-professionals?

Some—perhaps numbering 15 to 20—would prefer that the church hire a teaching pastor. "We take their comments seriously," Kotiuga says, "and evaluate their feedback on the preaching. We're not saying that we will never hire someone for such a role. But at this point, we are not ready to move in that direction."[69]

---

[67] Ibid.
[68] Ibid.
[69] Ibid.

Wild Goose Christian Community, Indian Valley, Floyd County, VA

| Greeting | **Encouraging** | **Spurring On** | **Teaching/Instructing** |
| Serving | Praying For | Confessing |

The small white meeting place of the Wild Goose Community is nestled among the hills and trees of Indian Valley in Southwestern Virginia. The 100-year-old church that had met here closed in 2012. Then, as part of the "1001 New Worshiping Communities" initiative sponsored by the Presbyterian Church USA, Edwin Lacy arrived in 2013. After extensively remodeling the building, he reopened its doors for the Wild Goose Community. Partly because of its attention-grabbing name and participatory meetings, National Public Radio (NPR) ran a story on it that aired throughout the United States. In an interview, Lacy told me how this Wild Goose flies.

What led to the Wild Goose name?

The population of Indian Valley traces its heritage to Scotch–Irish settlers. In Celtic theology the Wild Goose, not the dove, symbolizes the Holy Spirit. Like the Holy Spirit, life in this church tends to be free and unpredictable.

How did you change the traditional church building?

Although the original church windows remain, I covered the old paneling with sheetrock. The pews came out and were replaced by a circle of rocking chairs donated by people from surrounding churches. In place of the pulpit, we installed a fireplace with a simple wooden cross just above it. As one church member put it, "this house of worship is like an oversized

Appalachian living room with stained-glass windows." All these changes created a space in which the people could participate more freely.

Why did you shift to a participatory approach to congregational gatherings?

After seminary, I had preached the traditional monological sermon for many years. But I began to realize that the people themselves should be included in the process of expounding the gospel. I am not against monological preaching— there is a place for it. But it seemed to me that it excludes some real wisdom that Christians have to offer.

Further, here in the Wild Goose Community we are intentionally reaching out to the de-churched population, also called the "dones" or "church refugees." These people, often those who have grown up in church, left it decades ago and have not returned. Listening to one person telling them what to think or do often tops the list of what they typically do not like about traditional church. The de-churched make up about 60 percent of our congregation.

Why have you chosen not to meet on Sundays?

We meet on Tuesday evenings so that the other 40 percent can take part in churches that meet elsewhere on Sundays. From the start, I wanted to avoid being seen as competition by the other five or six churches here in Indian Valley. Then, too, we value the way the "churched" believers add stability and mentor those who had dropped out of church, helping them to get back into the swing of things. I also wanted to get away from Sunday mornings for the sake of those who have had bad associations with traditional church. Wild Goose Church is as "unchurchy" as possible.

We begin with a potluck dinner at 6:30. From there we move into the meeting room to celebrate Communion (we drink from Mason jars), followed by the church service itself, where we all sit in a circle in the rocking chairs. Instead of a stand-and-greet time, we begin by welcoming God, as each person around the circle tells one thing they are thankful to God for or one way they have seen God at work in nature or elsewhere. Our singing is also very participatory, as I select some songs while those in the congregation choose others. We have no piano or organ. Instead, I accompany the singing with my clawhammer banjo along with others playing fiddles and guitars.

With no monological sermon, how does teaching take place?

Although teaching is conversational, I preselect and carefully study a passage, examining its historical context and so on. In the meeting, I hand out single sheets of paper that contain the biblical text. After reading it out loud, I begin asking questions—usually five or six developed ahead of time. As the conversation unfolds, I will insert insights from my previous study where it makes sense to bring them in. But my intent is always: How does this Scripture impact our relationship with Jesus Christ and the way we live out that relationship? So the teaching is much more like a sermon than a Bible study. In a sense, everyone preaches together. The people are so eager to discuss, I don't always get through all the prepared questions.

In what other ways are Wild Goose meetings participatory?

We do contemplative prayer. Everyone does a centering exercise to calm our minds and hearts. I share a spoken prayer, and then we take from five to ten minutes of silence. Even though no one is saying anything, this is "participative silence."

How have the people responded to this way of "doing church"?

The conversational teaching method is the best-liked part of our meetings, followed by the contemplative prayer, and then the music. Occasionally I will do something different, omitting the discussion. But when I do, visitors often complain, disappointed that they did not get to experience it. One man wrote: "Wild Goose certainly has a different feel [than traditional church] and is not . . . as much of a performer–audience dynamic . . . more like family. . . . This is where my teenage daughter wants to come on Tuesday nights." He added that "the evening's topic usually fuels our conversation during the car ride home."

A Jewish woman wrote: "I attend Wild Goose to meet new people—the closest synagogue is Blacksburg, some 35 miles from me. Your format of dinner every week is most pleasurable and I have become more interested in the Bible because of the emphasis by so many people who live by the Bible."

Another wrote: "Wild Goose has brought Jesus alive for me again—up close and personal. The in-depth Scripture reading as well as the focus on how to really think about the Scripture and how it can influence your day-to-day life has made me feel closer to Jesus Christ."

You have spoken of spiritual "thin places." What do you mean by that?

In traditional Celtic Christianity, there are thin places, areas in which the veil between heaven and earth becomes mysteriously permeable, where physical and spiritual blend. We are now living in an industrial and technological world that has radically disassociated us with nature. The church today has the unique opportunity to create thin places in an over-stressed, fast-paced, lonely, and culturally homogenized world. Can thin places be made? No. But they can be prepared. The most crucial element of thin places is the presence of the Holy Spirit. And the Holy Spirit can be invited but never forced. Through the appreciation of God's creation, the celebration of who we are historically and culturally, and the intention of Christ-centered communion with one another, we can gather in hope, real hope, of the joining of the Holy Spirit—and of entering into a truly thin place.[70]

---

[70] Edwin Lacy, interview by author, January 11, 2016.

CHAPTER 7

Preparing the Congregation

The urban church today is faced with monumental challenges as it seeks to be God's reconciling witness. The urban congregation serves a transient population, much closer to the DNA of the early church that was focused on serving small groups of people rather than building beautiful cathedrals or mega malls. The call to hear God's voice and embrace the gifts of the Spirit is the basis of a life giving urban ecclesia. To be useful to God in a complex city environment requires fresh thinking and immediate divine action rather than a laborious following of an organizational protocol so common to the modern church. City congregations who help people find their calling and equip them to serve as ministers without resorting to special ordinations or licenses will provide a much needed oasis for others. When every member actualizes their God-given calling in the city all heaven breaks loose!

Jon Sharpe, C3 Leaders, Kirkland, WA,
Co-author with Ray Bakke, Street Signs: A New Direction in Urban Ministry

Asking those in a congregation to transition from spectating to participating in their main weekly meeting may meet stiff resistance to what will be perceived as a new way of doing church. Some might even label the proposal as a fad. Fads come and go, not only in popular culture but also in the church world. Trendy movements and hot topics, fueled by novelty, soon become passé and must give way to the next catchy emphasis. Interactive, participatory church, however, is anything but a passing whim. If it seems new, that is only because it is so old. True, practicing the priesthood of all believers in church gatherings fell out of fashion centuries ago. But it was the modus operandi in the New Testament church.

In Spencer Johnson's book, *Who Moved My Cheese?* the two little people, Hem and Haw, have run out of cheese. When Haw suggests they go in search of New Cheese, Hem declines: "No . . . I like it here. It's comfortable. It's what I know."[1] After Haw discovers another source of cheese and offers his friend some, Hem says, "I don't think I would like New Cheese. It's not what I'm used to. I want my *own* Cheese back and I'm not going to change until I get what I want"[2] Spectatoritis is what most church people, in Hem's words, are used to. And because they are comfortable with what they know, many will, like Hem, insist they are not going to change.

So for most churches any move to a participatory Sunday meeting must be done gently, gradually, and strategically. Everyone who has gone to church for any length of time will have deep-rooted beliefs about the way church must be done. Church traditions have molded us all to one degree or another. As a result wise leaders, before making any significant changes in the meeting format, will—with careful thought and prayer—prepare God's people with biblical teaching on several fronts. Such teaching will

---

[1] Spencer Johnson, *Who Moved My Cheese?* (New York: G. P. Putman's Sons, 1998), 41.
[2] Ibid. 61.

address the *why* questions, providing answers that undergird the *what* of participatory gathering.

This chapter will identify and briefly describe some of the areas of biblical instruction your congregation may need before you begin moving toward such a change. The *briefly* in the preceding sentence means just that. What follows is not meant to be exhaustive but suggestive.

Welcoming the Holy Spirit and His Gifts

One of the starkest contrasts between the Old and New Covenants is the presence of the Holy Spirit within everyone who becomes a child of God through faith in Christ. Again and again in the Old Testament we read that God's Spirit came upon this one and that one. That way of describing the operation of the Holy Spirit disappears in the New Testament. Instead, as Jesus—speaking of the Spirit—said, "he . . . will be in you" (John 14:17). Not *upon* but *in*. This truth is found repeatedly in the New Testament. Each Christ-follower is now a temple, a residence, of the Holy Spirit. This has radical implications for the shape of our meetings as well as for the way we help believers transition to one-anothering.

This living-in Holy Spirit arrives with gifts. Unlike Christmas presents given to delight and benefit the individual, these gifts are more like tools a builder provides to workers for completing a construction project. The clear teaching of the New Testament is that "a spiritual gift is given to each of us so we can help each other" (1 Cor. 12:7, NLT). And, "each one should use whatever gift he has received to serve others, faithfully administering God's grace in its various forms" (1 Peter 4:10). Paul urged Corinthian believers to "try to excel in gifts that build up the church" (1 Cor. 14:12). And when the church gathered, whatever the believer-workers did with their gift-tools was to be done "for the strengthening of the church" (v. 14). Today, though, non-participatory Sunday meetings assure those in the "audience" that the format will shield them from such responsibility. Their gifts may remain comfortably at rest in the unopened tool box.

A few years ago the Barna Group, summarizing a survey it had conducted on spiritual gifts, reported:

> Between those who do not know their gift (15%), those who say they don't have one (28%) and those who claimed gifts that are not biblical (20%), nearly two-thirds of the self-identified Christian population who claim to have heard about spiritual gifts have not been able to accurately apply whatever they have heard or what the Bible teaches on the subject to their lives.[3]

How much of this inability to accurately apply what they have learned about spiritual gifts can be explained by the lack of opportunity to practice using them when the church gathers? Imagine the results if construction workers were given cordless drills, pneumatic nail guns, and circular saws and told how the tools worked—but without any opportunity to practice boring holes, driving nails, or cutting two-by-fours. An apprenticeship in carpentry includes both teaching about the tools as well as hands-

---

[3] "Survey Describes the Spiritual Gifts That Christians Say They Have: Research Releases in Faith & Christianity," Barna Group, February 9, 2009, accessed April 18, 2016, https://www.barna.org/barna-update/faith-spirituality/211-survey-describes-the-spiritual-gifts-that-christians-say-they-have#.VuKcWjY-9YN.

on experience in using them. Discipleship in following Jesus and learning to help build his church should also include carefully structured opportunities to practice using the Spirit-given gifts.

Hearing God Speak

This Holy Occupant who lives in the houses of our human bodies is a resident teacher (John 14:26; 1 John 2:27). One of the main ways to prepare a congregation for participatory gatherings will be to help them discover how to listen with their inner, spiritual ears. Centuries of church practice have left far too many thinking God's main way of speaking to them today is through their outer, physical ears as they hear the live or recorded sermons of ordained professionals.

While serving as a pastor I communicated plans to begin asking the elders to share in the Sunday morning teaching. As I was explaining this during an annual meeting, one of the church members objected that he didn't want to come to church and hear teaching from his dentist. Imagine one of Cornelius's relatives or friends storming out of the meeting in his house (Acts 10), declaring, "I don't want to hear about spiritual things from a fisherman!" Sorry, Peter. Stick with your boats and nets.

If those in our churches are convinced God speaks to them only through pastors or preachers, a participatory meeting will seem not only pointless but wrong. Why? Because they will not believe they or their peers have anything of spiritual value to say to others. Like the boy Samuel, church people—whether young or old—need to learn how to recognize God's voice when he is speaking to them. I have encountered many Christians who, in spite of having attended church for decades, say wistfully, "I just wish God would speak to people today." The people in the Bible had an advantage over us, they think, because somewhere between Revelation 22:21 and now, God stopped talking.

In *The Allure of Gentleness*, Dallas Willard says, "One of the things I began to realize over time is that for many years God spoke to me and told me to do things, and I didn't know it was him. I just thought it was me thinking."[4] Willard elaborates:

> I believe the single most important thing I have to do is to encourage people to believe that God will speak to them and that they can come to understand and recognize his voice. . . . God speaks constantly to people, but most of them don't know what's happening. . . . Now, sometimes God does strange things to get people's attention, but the fundamental way God speaks to us is by causing thoughts in our mind that we come to learn to have a characteristic quality, content, and spirit about them. . . . I don't think we should rule out any options, but we should understand that God's preferred mode is to address willing hearers by the thoughts that are given to their minds, the 'still small voice' of I Kings 19:12 (KJV).[5]

But as has been said, many long-time church people operate under the assumption that God speaks to them only through clergy. One man asked God to speak to him personally through the pastor, so that whatever God wanted him to hear would come that way. This sounds eerily Old Covenant, as if he

---

[4] Dallas Willard, *The Allure of Gentleness: Defending the Faith in the Manner of Jesus* (New York: HarperCollins Publishers, 2015), 152.
[5] Ibid., 147-50.

sees the pastor as mediator between him and God. The man apparently thought that just as God spoke to Moses who then spoke to the people, God speaks today to the pastor and the pastor speaks to him. Certainly God can and does communicate with his people through pastors and others. But if the people think the pastor is God's only mouthpiece, they need careful teaching and equipping on hearing from God for themselves.

A Google search on the words "ask the pastor" (enclosed in quotation marks to search for just those words in that order) returned 338,000 links to websites. One ask-the-pastor site indicated that questions had been received and responded to on well over 100 subjects. But is even the wisest pastor an expert on that many subjects? Let us say the question involves marriage. Would it not be appropriate to hear from a Spirit-taught, mature Christian couple with 40 years of marital experience behind them? Or if the question involves money, what about the faithful elder who, in addition to having spent years counseling people as a financial advisor, has also learned to hear God speak?

Scripture, of course, must play key roles in all of this. First, knowing what God has said and how he has said it in the Bible tunes our spiritual ears to the sound of his voice. Just as we learned to know the voices of our parents by hearing them speak, attending to how God has spoken in Scripture equips us to distinguish his voice from other voices that bombard us. Second, whatever we believe God has spoken to us must be measured against the straightedge of biblical revelation.

So one of the major roles of a pastor or teacher will be to help people learn how to hear God speaking to them personally as well as speaking through them for the benefit of the church. That is the thrust of Ephesians 4:11-14, where the pastors and teachers are to equip people for their work of serving God and each other. Those in our churches today typically need help in learning how to tune their inner ears to hear God's still small voice. Hearing him is among the birthrights of a Christian under the New Covenant (Heb. 10:16; John 6:45; 10:27). And if what members of Christ's body contribute during participatory meetings is to have any value, such hearing is essential. The first line of a classic hymn had it right: "Lord, speak to me that I may speak in living echoes of Thy tone."

Practicing the Priesthood of All Believers

If you were to survey a hundred Christians asking, "Do you think of yourself as a priest?" how many yeses would you expect? How often have you spoken of other Christ-followers as "my fellow Christians?" Imagine the raised eyebrows if you were to address them as "my fellow priests." Yet Martin Luther once wrote about his hope that "this word 'priest' should become as common as the word Christian."[6]

Today, when we think of the word *priest*, images of clerical collars, cassocks, and silk skullcaps may come to mind. The Hebrew word *kohen* is translated *priest* in English versions of the Old Testament. According to the 1961 edition of *Unger's Bible*

---

[6] Martin Luther, *The Epistles of St. Peter and St. Jude: Preached and Explained* (New York, NY: Anson D.F. Randolph, 1859), 106, quoted in "The Priesthood of All Believers," Dr. Art Lindsley, Institute for Faith, Works & Economics, October 15, 2013, accessed April 18, 2016, https://tifwe.org/resource/the-priesthood-of-all-believers/.

Dictionary, "there is no consensus . . . as to the etymology of the Heb. *Kohen.*"⁷ Unger goes on to say, though, that one scholar linked it to an Arabic root word meaning to *draw near.* This would square nicely with the fact that only the ancient Jewish priests could draw near to God. As the Lord warned Aaron, "But only you and your sons may serve as priests in connection with everything at the altar and inside the curtain. I am giving you the service of the priesthood as a gift. Anyone else who comes near the sanctuary must be put to death" (Num. 18:7).

If *priest* does come from a root meaning to *draw near,* that also helps explain the New Testament priesthood of all believers. Christ, our Great High Priest, has drawn near to God and now sits at his right hand. And because we believers are in Christ, we too are given the privilege to "draw near to God" (Heb. 10:22) and to "come near to God" (Jas. 4:8). In Christ, we have rights of access which, under the Old Covenant, only priests—particularly the high priest—enjoyed.

After the close of the New Testament, it did not take long for the current of historical drift to carry this revolutionary priesthood truth far beyond the reach of most believers. As Greg Ogden writes, "even though the Bible knows no distinction between clergy and laity, the separation between the classes developed relatively early in the history of the church."⁸ By the

---

⁷ Merrill F. Unger, *Unger's Bible Dictionary* (Chicago, IL: Moody Press, 1961), 882.

⁸ Greg Ogden, *The New Reformation: Returning the Ministry to the People of God* (Grand Rapids: Zondervan Publishing House, 1990), 66.

fourth century, he says, "the distinction between clergy and laity [had] become full-blown."[9]

Although Martin Luther and other reformers recovered this truth of the priesthood of believers, in the centuries since then—even in Protestant churches—it has gotten far more lip-service than legwork. The doctrine shapes our church meetings about as much as an exhibit of horse-drawn buggies in a museum affects our daily drive to work. In *When You Come Together*, Amy S. Anderson writes, "many pastors who teach about the priesthood of all believers fail to train their people to do priestly ministry."[10]

Art Lindsley laments the neglect of this biblical truth after its rediscovery in the sixteenth century:

> There is an important biblical idea that has great implications for our personal spirituality and public life in the Church and in the world: the idea that every believer is a priest, regardless of his or her full-time occupation. This notion was one of the top three ideas of the Protestant Reformation. The first two, Sola Scriptura—which asserts the sole authority of Scripture—and Sola Fide—which teaches justification by faith alone—have been widely taught, but the notion of the "priesthood of all believers" has been by far the most neglected.[11]

Teaching believers to think of themselves as priests must include teaching them not to think of themselves as laypeople. In *The Jesus Way*, Eugene H. Peterson writes,

---

[9] Ibid.

[10] Amy Anderson, *When You Come Together: Challenging the Church to an Interactive Relationship with God* (Being Church, 2010), 83.

[11] Lindsley.

Within the Christian community there are few words that are more disabling than "layperson" and "laity." The words convey the impression—an impression that quickly solidifies into a lie—that there is a two-level hierarchy among the men and women who follow Jesus. There are those who are trained, sometimes referred to as the called, the professionals who are paid to preach, teach, provide guidance in the Christian way, occupying the upper level. The lower level is made up of everyone else, those whom God assigned jobs as storekeepers, lawyers, journalists, parents, and computer programmers. . . . It is a barefaced lie, insinuated into the Christian community by the devil (who has an established reputation for using perfectly good words for telling lies).[12]

The two-tiered notion that distinguishes clergy from laity comes not from the New Testament but from church tradition. Such split-level thinking creates a paternalistic environment that fosters the comfortable tendency for believers to live as dependents rather than to press on toward maturity. Parenting is God's temporary gift to infants, toddlers, and children. In his church, however, Jesus warns us against setting up a religious parenting environment. On the negative side, he said, "do not call anyone on earth 'father,' for you have one Father, and he is in heaven" (Matt. 23:9). (The context is not parents in normal families but leaders in religious settings.) And on the positive side: "you are all brothers" (Matt. 23:8). No mention of super-siblings!

---

[12] Eugene Peterson, *The Jesus Way: A Conversation on the Ways That Jesus Is the Way* (Grand Rapids, MI: William B. Eerdmans Publishing Co, 2011), 11.

Religious titles widen and reinforce the clergy–laity divide. Where does the New Testament ever authorize the title reverend for any church leader? The King James Version uses the word reverend (Hebrew, yaré) just once—in a description of God (Psa. 111:9). The NIV—which never uses the term reverend—translates yaré as awesome. Such adjectival clothing is far too large to fit any sinful human being!

When it comes to church leadership, religious titles are conspicuously absent in the New Testament. Today we refer to Paul as the Apostle Paul, using apostle as a title. By contrast, he referred to himself as Paul, an apostle, using apostle as a role description. In contemporary church culture, we reserve religious titles exclusively for clergy. If Robert is a pastor, he is Pastor Robert. But in the same church if Janet is a teacher, no one addresses her as Teacher Janet. Jesus warned against using the world's methods to make people feel leadership's "weight of authority" (Matt. 20:25, NEB).

Several years ago the pastor of our church asked me to plant a church—which I did. A few years after that, the denomination's district superintendent began pressing me to be ordained. This created a crisis for me. On the one hand, I cringed at the thought of driving the clergy-laity wedge between me and my brothers and sisters in Christ. On the other hand, I did not want to be insubordinate. So—reluctantly—I finally agreed to ordination and was dubbed a reverend. After retirement, I enrolled in a graduate school to pursue a doctoral degree, not for the title but so that I could teach the theology of work for the school. After I had received the degree, a church asked me to speak on a Sunday morning. Much to my dismay, the reader board on the busy road in front of the building presented me as The Rev. Dr. Larry Peabody. That hurt.

Part of preparing God's people to participate when they meet with other believers will include instruction on seeing themselves as priests. A willingness to drop religious titles and unbiblical layperson labels from the church vocabulary will demonstrate the sincerity of such instruction.

Discovering Calling

Curing Christians of chronic spectatoritis will require treatment that incorporates a biblical understanding of calling. Far too many in church circles think of the call to ministry as a divine summons that comes only to a few—namely professionals in church-related roles. Paul Stevens describes this exclusive understanding of calling by noting that "almost the only people who speak of being 'called of God' are 'full-time' missionaries and pastors."[13]

This shrunken concept of calling creates the perception that only a tiny percentage of Christians are called to ministry. This idea gets reinforced on Sunday if the pastor and other professionals carry out essentially all the ministry to and for the gathered believers. When those in the "audience" see themselves as the uncalled, passivity naturally results. Correcting this unbiblical understanding requires relearning the way we think about two words—*call* and *ministry*.

---

[13] Stevens, *The Other Six Days*, 72.

Call

In his book, *The Call,* Os Guinness describes four ways the Bible uses the word *call.* First, just as we do today, Scripture uses it in the sense of calling out to someone else—as in when you call someone to come and help you. Second, it sometimes means "to name, and to name means to call into being or to make."[14] Third, the New Testament uses it to mean nearly the same thing as salvation—as in "those he called, he also justified; those he justified, he also glorified" (Rom. 8:30). Fourth, in addition to calling people to himself to belong to him, "Jesus . . . also calls them to other things and tasks: to peace, to fellowship, to eternal life, to suffering, and to service."[15]

Guinness then speaks of the third and fourth meanings as our primary and secondary callings. "Our primary calling as followers of Christ is by him, to him, and for him. . . . Our secondary calling . . . is that everyone, everywhere, and in everything should think, speak, live, and act entirely for him."[16] It becomes clear, then, that every Christ-follower has been called by God. He does not limit his call to those in some form of church work or to what has come to be known as full-time Christian service. All of us are called to belong to God and to serve him 24/7.

Ministry

The NIV translates the New Testament word *diakonia* (from which we get our word *deacon*) sometimes as *ministry* and

---

[14] Os Guinness, *The Call: Finding and Fulfilling the Central Purpose of Your Life* (Nashville, TN: Word Publishing, 1998), 30.
[15] Ibid.
[16] Ibid., 31.

sometimes as *service*. So it speaks of serving in whatever capacity. For example, Paul uses the same word to describe his own work as an apostle (2 Cor. 4:1) as he does to describe the work for which all believers need to be prepared (Eph. 4:12). Just as God calls all believers to himself, he also calls all of us to ministry, to service for him.

Too often Christians hear those in so-called "full-time service" say something like, "I left secular work to go into the ministry." But think about what those words imply: "I left work that was *not* ministry to do work that *is* ministry." Further, this suggests that any Christian who wants to do ministry (to serve) must resign from work that helps people flourish and cares for God's creation. However, the truth is that God sends many of his people to minister (serve) as public school teachers, farmers, accountants, programmers, financial advisors, and so on.

As in so many other areas of the Christian life, getting our vocabulary right is critically important, because the terms we use become the tools we think with. Just as a hammer is the wrong tool for fixing a leaky pipe, the wrong word can never repair a damaging idea. Does this mean we should expunge the word *ministry* from our lexicon? Not at all. Instead we need to extend *ministry* (service) so that it applies to all forms of God-honoring work. In addition to the ministry of the Word, there is the ministry of education, the ministry of construction, the ministry of automotive repair, and on it goes. Many governments in the world use the word in this way. Spain has a Ministry of Public Works and Transport; Ontario a Ministry of Labour; Japan a Ministry of Agriculture, Forestry and Fisheries. In each case, those working for these agencies minister to (serve) the public in their designated fields.

Consider the effect if believers come to a Sunday meeting with the hurtful idea that there is just one minister to whom they should look to carry out the ministry. In that case, any suggestion that they are all ministers called of God to minister to each other in that setting will meet resistance. This helps to explain why spectatoritis has persisted in the church century after century. Curing it includes helping a congregation transition to participatory gatherings through careful instruction in the New Testament truth about calling.

Understanding the Biblical Role of Pastors

Does the New Testament recognize the need for pastors in the Church? Absolutely. Pastors, says Paul in Ephesians 4:11, are among those given to the Church to prepare believers for the work God has called them to do. That kind of shepherding is needed today as much as when Paul wrote those words.

But centuries of tradition exert a powerful sway on today's Christians when it comes to the way they see the role of pastors. A few examples will illustrate some of the ways this influence surfaces. When I served as a pastor, more than once someone remarked that I was the head of that local church. Some church members, if hospitalized, do not consider having been visited unless it was the pastor who comes calling. Churches often require that the pastor be an ex officio (because of one's position or station) member of all boards and committees. Other congregations are persuaded only the pastor can preach, conduct weddings, baptize, or officiate during Communion. How many of the ideas just mentioned in this paragraph have New Testament support? None.

So transitioning to a participatory church meeting may well require some remedial education for a congregation. Pastors—along with other church leaders—do have an important role in a one-anothering church meeting. But that responsibility differs widely from the traditionally written and commonly understood job description. Ephesians 4:11-12 makes that role clear. Pastors, along with other church leaders, are "to prepare God's people for works of service, so that the body of Christ may be built up." Pastors, then, are to ready Christians for doing the various kinds of serving-others work in the Church.

For contemporary congregations, the work of athletic coaches makes a good illustration, because in many ways that work parallels the biblical role of pastors. In football, when game-time arrives, coaches are not doing their work out on the field. Instead, a great deal of it has been done behind the scenes. They communicate what they know of how to play the game. They devise ways to make certain players are physically fit for action. They nurture teamwork and interdependency. And they provide plenty of practice to prepare players for what they will do out on the gridiron. The pastors-as-coaches theme shows up repeatedly in many of the church practice examples in Chapter Six.

Years ago E. Stanley Jones, twentieth-century missionary to India, recognized pastoral coaching as a powerful antidote to spectatoritis: "The laity must come out of the stands as spectators and take the field as players; and the clergy . . . must come off the field as players and take the sidelines as coaches of a team. The clergy . . . must be the guides, stimulators, and spiritualizers of an essentially lay movement."[17]

But when it comes to the pastoral gift, church tradition and practice work against participatory gatherings in another way—by changing a New Testament plural to singular. Listen carefully to what church people say when talking about their church, and you will typically hear them speak of the pastor (individual) not of the pastors (team). Yet in the New Testament, the prevailing examples show us pastors/elders/shepherds serving in partnership.

David Watson comments on this plural pattern: "Although there might have been a presiding elder, there is never the slightest hint of a solitary leader (such as the pastor) even in the smallest and youngest churches. Always it was a shared responsibility, thereby giving much mutual encouragement, protection, and support."[18] Many of the churches represented in Chapter Six operate not with solo pastors but with pastoral teams that rotate the teaching responsibility.

In a church of 50 or 100 people, the Holy Spirit has probably implanted the pastoral gift in more than one person. The challenge, then, is three-fold: (a) to discover who the pastors are, (b) to equip them for the work God has called them to do in and for the church, and (c) to teach the whole church to recognize and welcome the pastoral leadership of them all.

One pastor placed the names of those he knew could preach and teach on what he called his emergency list—emergency

---

[17] Jones, 147.
[18] David Watson, *I Believe in the Church* (Grand Rapids, MI: Eerdmans Pub. Co., 1979), 271.

meaning when he was ill or out of town. But if the absence of one member of the body for one Sunday constitutes an emergency, what message does that communicate? For those who have been solo pastors for years, Greg Ogden may have identified the most difficult element of the transition to participatory meetings: "The true test of shared ministry is the ability to open up the power center—the pulpit—to others."[19]

Serving the Church in Both Its Modes

Preparing believers for participatory gatherings should include instruction in the two modes of church life. As discussed in Chapter Three, *church* to most Christians today brings to mind the church service when the congregation gathers for its weekly meeting in the church building. That assembly, the gathered church, is a very important mode of the church's existence, but it is only one mode. In most churches, the assembled body spends less than one percent of its time in its gathered form. During the other ninety-nine percent it lives and moves as the scattered church—in homes, neighborhoods, workplaces, and so on.

We see the scattered church at work in Acts: "On that day a great persecution broke out against the church at Jerusalem, and all except the apostles were scattered throughout Judea and Samaria. . . .Those who had been scattered preached the word wherever they went" (Acts 8:1, 4). The church continued to be the church even while scattered. In fact, only in its dispersed mode could the church accomplish God's Kingdom purposes in the

---

[19] Ogden, 179.

world at large. And the work of the Kingdom "out there" was done not by the apostles but by the other members of the body.

Scattered translates a Greek word rooted in *diaspora*. It means to sow, as in scattering seed throughout a field. In one of his parables, Jesus speaks of sowing the "sons of the kingdom" throughout the world-field like seed (Matt. 13:37, 38). In the Old Testament diaspora (dispersion), Daniel was one of those seeds God scattered into a workplace, right into the idolatrous core of the government in Babylon. In that pagan context, Daniel took root, grew, and bore fruit for God. Today, in addition to knowing themselves as priests, Christians need to see themselves as seeds—life-carrying cells flung into the world to carry out God's agenda where they live, work, and play.

Our word *church* has become so strongly identified with the gathered congregation, many believers find it difficult to think of themselves as still in church while scattered into those situations where life has placed them. As part of preparing a congregation for meaningful participation, the gathered church should include teaching that assures believers that, as members of Christ's body, they are never out of church.

How do the gathered and scattered modes relate to each other? What takes place when the church gathers should prepare its members for that far larger block of scattered time. In other words, the thrust of gathered church meetings should be *centrifugal*, "acting in a direction *away from* a center."[20] Sadly,

---

[20] *Merriam-Webster Dictionary*, s.v. "centrifugal," accessed April 18, 2016, http://www.merriam-webster.com/dictionary/centrifugal.

far too many Sunday sessions are *centripetal*, "acting in a direction *toward* a center."[21] NASA's astronaut training program is centrifugal. Yes, the preparation phase involves a certain amount of centripetal force—classroom learning that takes place "in here." But even these activities are oriented toward preparing the trainees for the work they'll do "out there." If selected after basic training, candidates are linked with veteran astronauts who share their knowledge and experience.

In gathered-church meetings, believers need to hear both from those with preaching/teaching gifts as well as from those with knowledge and experience in every phase of scattered-church life. In most cases, a pastor serving full time on a church payroll has limited experience with what confronts people in, say, the ethical dilemmas of a contemporary workplace. For this reason, the meeting format of the gathered church should provide opportunities for reports from the scattered church. How has God been moving in this ethically challenged workplace, that conflict-torn neighborhood, or those alienated families?

In any transition toward more participation in the gathered church, Christians need to understand both modes of the church—their roles, their importance, and how each relates to the other.

Seeing All of Life through the Kingdom Lens

In his now much-quoted inauguration manifesto given in the Free University of Amsterdam, Abraham Kuyper said, "There

---

[21] *Merriam-Webster Dictionary, s.v.* "centripetal," accessed April 18, 2016, http://www.merriam-webster.com/dictionary/centripetal.

is not a square inch in the whole domain of human existence over which Christ, who is sovereign over all, does not cry 'Mine!'"[22] Yet many Christians, conditioned by centuries of religious tradition, see church-related matters as "his," belonging to Jesus, and almost everything else as "its," belonging to the world. In other words, they believe God cares about so-called sacred zones but is indifferent (or even opposed) to anything secular. Any transition to participatory church meetings should include instruction to correct this defect in vision. We might describe the condition as spiritual diplopia, the visual disorder in which one object appears as two.

The single object is God's Kingdom. The dualistic and unbiblical sacred–secular divide causes it to appear as two. God's Kingdom—his sovereign authority to rule—extends over his entire creation. Scripture opens with a plain assertion of fact: "In the beginning, God created the heavens and the earth" (Gen. 1:1). The *Expositor's Bible Commentary* explains that the words, *the heavens and the earth*, are "a figure of speech . . . for the expression of 'totality'. . . equivalent to the 'all things' in Isa. 44:24."[23] As Creator, God naturally is the rightful Ruler of the "all things" he has made. The Psalmist links the Lord's kingship with the entire planet (Psa. 47:2, 47:7-8). Jesus affirmed this truth, calling his Father, "Lord of heaven and earth" (Matt. 11:25).

---

[22] Dr. Abraham Kuyper, "Sphere Sovereignty," October 20, 1880, quoted in Richard J. Mouw, *Abraham Kuyper: A Short and Personal Introduction* (Grand Rapids, MI: Wm. B. Eerdmans Publishing Co., 2011), 4.
[23] Frank E. Gaebelein, (Gen. Ed.). *The Expositor's Bible Commentary*, vol. 2 (Grand Rapids: Zondervan Publishing House, 1990), 23.

The sacred–secular divide helps to explain the historical drift away from participatory church gatherings. Because the reason for meeting has long been presented as worship (see Chapter Two), only "sacred" things seem worthy of the agenda: sermons, prayer, spiritual songs, church-authorized programs, missions, and the like. "Secular" concerns—public school issues, ethical choices on the job, government, law, politics—will only sully the pristine atmosphere of worship. So most of the congregation, whose daily lives have immersed them in secular concerns, seemingly cannot offer much that is worshipful in the worship service.

Recognizing and Reporting on the Providence of God

Participatory church meetings can be enriched as believers tell faith stories or bring reports from the front on how they have seen the providence of God in their daily lives. But how well does the typical twenty-first century Christian understand the biblical teaching about God's providence? In a lecture on "Creation and Providence," R. C. Sproul said, "Christians on the one hand defend the doctrine of creation but on the other hand remain almost silent on the doctrine of divine providence." [24] To put it another way, much teaching about God presents him as creator and redeemer, but little is said concerning God as provider and sustainer.

---

[24] R. C. Sproul, "Creation and Providence" (lecture, Ligonier Leadership Conference, 2009) quoted in Robert Rothwell, "Forgotten Providence - Ligonier Leadership Conference (I)," Ligonier Ministries, October 20, 2009, accessed April 18, 2016, http://www.ligonier.org/blog/forgotten-providence-ligonier-leadership-conference-i/.

Only occasionally—perhaps rarely—will any of us see God at work in a genuine miracle. But eyes that are spiritually alert and expectant will see God's providential hand at work all the time and everywhere. Whatever our age, financial state, or education, all of us are experts at watching. We watch for opportunities, for trends, and for storms, but how often do we watch for God? All of us know about bird-watching, whale-watching, and weight-watching, but how much do we know about God-watching?

Once God's people learn to watch him at work in their homes, jobs, and neighborhoods, they will have plenty to share that will encourage and spur on fellow believers. One means of preparing God's people to keep an eye out for his activity is to remind them of the ways in which he has, in Scripture, revealed himself as working. For example, he reconciles enemies, forgives wrongs, meets needs, heals illnesses, restores after brokenness, directs steps, governs events, answers prayer, sets free, and grants favor even from opponents. This list could be expanded many times over.

The God who worked in Bible times still works today. What God-produced opportunity has come along for sharing what Christ has done? How has God used a particular Scripture passage in the process of making a critical decision? What fresh answer to prayer has a family received?

God does much of his providential work through us, the earth-managers he delegated to "rule . . . over all the earth" (Gen. 1:26). As Martin Luther put it in his "Exposition of Psalm 147":

> God could easily give you grain and fruit without your plowing and planting. But He does not want to do so. . . . What else is all our work to God—whether in the fields, in the garden,

in the city, in the house, in war, or in government—but just such a child's performance, by which He wants to give His gifts in the fields, at home, and everywhere else? These are the masks of God, behind which He wants to remain concealed and do all things.[25]

Congregations need to be taught how to see behind the masks of God. How and through whom has God brought about reconciliation with a coworker who has wronged a believer—or vice versa? What circumstances and people did God employ in releasing a young person from a drug habit? Who has God sent to provide for the needs of others? Accounts like this, related before the entire congregation—in person or by means of a video recording—can demonstrate how God still works in and through the lives of his people today.

The Holy Spirit and his gifts, hearing God speak, the priesthood of all believers, calling, the role of pastors, serving the church in both its modes, seeing all of life through the Kingdom lens, and recognizing and reporting on the providence of God— these are some of the teaching areas that will lay a sound foundation for participatory gatherings.

Reasonable Reminders

In addition to biblical teaching, preparing the congregation for participation in the main weekly meeting will require some

---

[25] Martin Luther, *Luther's Works,* Vol. 14, quoted in J. D. Greear, "Martin Luther on the 'Masks of God,'" August 5, 2013, accessed April 18, 2016, http://www.jdgreear.com/my_weblog/2013/08/martin-luther-on-gods-masks.html.

pragmatic measures and instructions as well. A friend related that a leader in his church, after finishing his message, asked if anyone wanted to comment. The people were caught completely by surprise. This had not happened before, so they were unprepared. Many in the congregation could not hear the three who spoke. One of those droned on and on. Observing a few common-sense guidelines can forestall such deterrents to participation:

1. Factor the size of your meeting room, its acoustics, and the number in the congregation into the decision of whether those who speak need a microphone.

2. Establish a few simple rules for those who make comments or ask questions. For example:

   a. Speak clearly. If using a microphone, hold it close to your mouth. If you have no microphone, project your voice to those farthest from you.

   b. Make certain that whatever you say will strengthen or encourage others in their faith and service.

   c. Share only what is appropriate. Never criticize another person or another faith.

   d. Be brief. Yield to others who may wish to speak as well.

(In Appendix B one pastor describes his experience in transitioning from the typical church-meeting format to participatory gatherings.)

The Magnitude of Making the Transition

Practicing life together as a body will require some major paradigm shifts in the way all of us see ourselves—whatever our role in the meeting. The reality is that audience mode, while providing some sense of being together, allows us to assemble with our individualism unchallenged. Audience mode allows me to come and go with little or no perception of responsibility for the other spectators. Audience mode provides slight if any opportunity to lay down my life for others or to risk using my Spirit-given gifts. Audience mode means that, in spite of some surface socializing, I am free to leave just as isolated and self-absorbed as I arrived.

One-anothering—loving each other as Jesus loves us— takes us in the opposite direction. Spectatoritis loses its power to paralyze as participation carries out its healing effect. When each part has opportunity to do its work for the rest of the body, we will discover how to connect our faith with our voices. If in our gathering together we have not learned how to witness to each other, how can we be expected in our scattering to witness to the world?

APPENDIX A:

FaithStory Presentation Guidelines,

Northwood Church, Maple Grove, MN

Thanks for being willing to share your FaithStory at Northwood Church! Your FaithStory is a great opportunity to tell people how Jesus Christ has changed your life and the people who hear your FaithStory are genuinely encouraged and challenged!

Here are some guidelines to assist you in preparing and sharing your FaithStory.

1. Prayer: Begin with prayer asking God to help you in this process.
2. Content: Please make clear how you came to believe in Jesus Christ and/or how you are sharing your faith with others.
   a. Be authentic – be you!
   - Tell your story the way it happened – be real!
   - Resist the temptation to compare your story with other FaithStories.

- Don't embellish your story or dwell excessively on past sins.

  b. Be intentional.

- Identify one main idea or theme you want to communicate through your FaithStory.

- Always enhance the reputation of Jesus Christ. He is the one who has changed your life and given you forgiveness of sin and eternal life!

- Refrain from criticizing or putting down people, groups, churches, etc.

  c. Be concise.

- Avoid clichés and language that sound overly religious, i.e. "salvation", "scripture" (use "the Bible").

- Make it interesting. Begin with a "hook," i.e. a question, statement, or common experience that makes people want to listen to you.

- Keep your story less than 5 minutes in length (1 1/4 to 1 1/3 pages, single spaced, 12 pt. font).

- Think in chapters or blocks such as: 1) what my life was like before I became a Christian 2) how I became a Christian 3) how Jesus has changed my life since I decided to follow Him.

- Remember this is your FaithStory, not your life story! Be wise and let Christ shine through you.

3. Place and Time: On Sunday, be in the Community Center meeting room by 9:00 a.m.

4. Dress: Wear something you feel comfortable in ("business casual").

5.   Preparation: Send a written draft to Brian approximately two weeks before your Faith Story date. Schedule a meeting with Brian to review your Faith Story.[1]

---

[1] Brian Doten, email message to author, July 1, 2015.

APPENDIX B:

Our Journey in Implementing Participatory Meetings

By Brian Anderson

When I arrived at Milpitas Bible Fellowship in 1990, our meetings were fairly typical of most other churches. After thirty to forty minutes of worship, I would give the announcements, preach my sermon, and pronounce the closing benediction. We experienced little if any real interaction and mutual body ministry during our meetings. The whole church looked to me as its source of edification. When God began opening my eyes to the importance of participatory church meetings, my first reaction was one of fear. I was terrified at what might happen if I truly opened up the meetings for all of God's people to minister. I feared our meetings would turn into bedlam if I gave all an opportunity to speak. I wrestled with these principles for some time until the strength of conviction overcame my fears.

In the summer of 1996, we began implementing these principles. Our first step was to open up various homes during the week for "house church" meetings. These "house churches" functioned as small group meetings for believers where each could learn to interact, pray, encourage, exhort, and minister to one another. Almost everyone was enthused about these home meetings, although at first we were a bit unsure how to function in them.

After a few months, as we became more comfortable with these informal home meetings, we began introducing more participation into our Sunday gatherings. I informed the congregation that anyone could participate by reading Scripture, praying during a lull in our praise singing, or starting a song that was on their heart. I brought the podium down from the platform to the lower level so that I could be closer to the people, thereby encouraging mutual interaction. We rearranged the chairs into concentric semi-circles so that we could look into one another's faces when speaking, instead of the back of someone's head. We bought a wireless microphone and began passing it around to those desiring to share what God had been doing in their lives or to encourage us by declaring what God had been teaching them from His Word. Sometimes these sessions included exhortations, admonitions, teachings, or the sharing of blessings or burdens. One woman revealed that she had recently been diagnosed with cancer. This allowed the whole church the opportunity to tangibly express their love and commitment by gathering around, laying hands on her, and praying. These changes felt a bit awkward at first. We had no previous model to guide us, and thus, felt a bit uncomfortable with them. Before long, however, many began contributing some very edifying insights and exhortations.

Furthermore we began opening up our meetings directly after the sermon for questions, comments, and insights from others. I was very hesitant about this new move, fearing that all doctrinal purity might be lost if everyone was permitted to comment from the Scriptures. On the contrary, this new aspect of our meetings proved especially enriching. Often someone would bring an insight that I had missed in my sermon preparation that would open up the text in an important way. At other times, people shared insights as to how they could personally apply the text under consideration. On still other occasions, someone would ask a question that many others had on their mind, but would not have voiced. Instead of producing doctrinal confusion, I found that the questions and comments enabled me to allay confusion by addressing the real issues which were perplexing the church. On those rare occasions when someone stated something unbiblical, I was able to gently refocus the church by bringing them back to Scripture. Instead of producing chaos, I discovered that it fostered spiritual maturity, intimacy, and love for the brethren. In fact, by adding the time of questions and comments, the church was easily able to concentrate on the Word of God for well over an hour. Often this segment proved to be the most invigorating and helpful of the entire meeting. Whereas our previous meetings lasted about ninety minutes, the new participatory meetings usually took a minimum of two hours to complete. The consensus of the church, though, was that the quality of the meetings was well worth the additional time spent together. The new meetings began to spawn additional interaction among the people. Many began going out to eat after the meeting to spend more time together. Sometimes up to half of the church could be seen piling into a Taco Bell, Burger King, or McDonald's after a Sunday morning meeting to continue their discussion of the things of God.

I cannot overstate the importance of creating an atmosphere of freedom for body participation in the meetings of the church. When church members do nothing but sit, listen, and take notes week after week for years on end, they tend to stagnate spiritually. Spiritual growth requires us to flex our spiritual muscles and apply the truths we are learning. What good is it for our people to learn that God wants them to use their spiritual gifts, exhort one another, bear each other's burdens, and rejoice with those who rejoice if we make no provision for them to do that when the church meets?

Having been involved in participatory church meetings now for almost two years, I know that I would find the traditional model stifling and unsatisfying. God has proven over and over that as we step out in obedience to apply the patterns we see in His Word, His blessings are sure to follow.[2]

---

[2] Reprinted by permission from Brian Anderson, "Discovering Participatory Church Meetings," Milpitas Bible Fellowship, accessed April 18, 2016, http://www.solidrock.net/library/anderson/essays/discovering.participatory.church.meetings.php.

REFERENCES

Anderson, A. (2010). When You Come Together: Challenging the Church to an Interactive Relationship with God. Being Church.

Anderson, B. (n.d.). Discovering Participatory Church Meetings. [Web log post]. Retrieved April 18, 2016, from http://www.solidrock.net/library/anderson/essays/discovering.participatory.church.meetings.php

Axiom Church. (n.d.). Our Story. Retrieved May 7, 2016, from http://axiomchurchny.com/about-us/our-story

Bakke, D. W. (2005). Joy at Work: A Revolutionary Approach to Fun on the Job Seattle, WA: PVG.

Banks, R. (1994). Paul's Idea of Community. Peabody, MA: Hendrickson Publishers, Inc.

Banks, R., & Banks, J. (1998). The Church Comes Home. Peabody, MA: Hendrickson Publishers, Inc.

Barna Group. (2009). Survey Describes the Spiritual Gifts that Christians Say They Have. [Research Releases in Faith & Christianity]. Retrieved April 18, 2016, from https://www.barna.org/barna-update/faith-spirituality/211-survey-describes-the-spiritual-gifts-that-christians-say-they-have#.VuKcWjY-9YN

Barna Group. (2009). Barna Studies the Research, Offers a Year-in-Review Perspective. [Research Releases in Faith and Christianity]. Retrieved April 18, 2016, from https://www.barna.org/barna-update/faith-spirituality/325-barna-studies-the-research-offers-a-year-in-review-perspective#.VudfZOaulSB

Barna Group. (2011). Six Reasons Young Christians Leave Church [Research Releases in Millennials & Generations]. Retrieved April 16, 2016, from https://www.barna.org/barna-update/millennials/528-six-reasons-young-christians-leave-church#.VuG76TY-9YO

Barna Group. (2013). 5 Reasons Millennial Stay Connected to Church. [Research Releases in Millennials & Generations]. Retrieved April 16, 2016, from https://www.barna.org/barna-update/millennials/635-5-reasons-millennials-stay-connected-to-church.html#.VudCWuaulSB

Bell, M. (2009, July 13). What Is An Average Church? [Web log post]. Retrieved April 16, 2016, from http://www.internetmonk.com/archive/michael-bell-what-is-an-average-church

Bichler, R. (Speaker) (2013, March 31). Rachel's FaithStory [Audio Podcast]. Retrieved April 12, 2016, from http://northwood.cc/2013/04/11/rachels-faithstory-4-7-2013/

Biesalski, C. (n.d.). The Less Routine, the More Life: How to Kill Monotony [Web log post]. Retrieved April 18, 2016, from http://www.alifeofblue.com/routine/

Block, P. (1993). Stewardship: Choosing Service over Self-Interest. San Francisco, CA: Berrett-Koehler Publishers, Inc.

Bonhoeffer, D. (1954). Life Together: A Discussion of Christian Fellowship. New York, NY: Harper & Row, Publishers.

Cordle, S. (2006, June 12). Why Don't More People Attend Small Groups? [Web log post]. Retrieved April 16, 2016, from http://www.smallgroups.com/articles/2006/why-dont-more-people-attend-small-groups.html?paging=off

Drane, J. (2001). The McDonaldization of the Church: Consumer Culture and the Church's Future. Macon, GA: Smyth & Helwys Publishing, Incorporated.

English, T. R. (October-November, 1900). The Decline of the Pulpit. The Union Seminary Magazine, October/November (Volume XII, 1900). Retrieved April 15, 2016, from https://books.google.co.in/books?id=KQEaAAAAYAAJ&pg=PA307&lpg=PA307&dq=%22pulpit+stars%22&source=bl&ots=Kn3Lr2IQIV&sig=rg-hbAVVKzutEj2KNw70EIvBWIw&hl=en&sa=X&redir_esc=y#v=onepage&q=%22pulpit%20stars%22&f=false

Gaebelein, F. E. (Gen. Ed.). (1990). The Expositor's Bible Commentary, vol. 2 Grand Rapids: Zondervan Publishing House.

Gordon-Conwell Theological Seminary. (2015, January). Christianity 2015: Religious Diversity and Personal Contact. International Bulletin of Missionary Research, Vol. 39, No. 1. Retrieved April 19, 2016, from http://www.gordonconwell.edu/ockenga/research/documents/1IBMR2015.pdf

Grady, J. L. (2014, April 2). 7 Reasons We Don't Make Disciples [Web log post]. Retrieved April 16, 2016, from http://www.charismamag.com/blogs/fire-in-my-bones/20101-7-reasons-we-don-t-make-disciples

Greear, J. D. (2013, August 5). Martin Luther on the Masks of God [Web log post]. Retrieved April 18, 2016, from http://www.jdgreear.com/my_weblog/2013/08/martin-luther-on-gods-masks.html

Guinness, O. (1998). The Call: Finding and Fulfilling the Central Purpose of Your Life. Nashville, TN: Word Publishing.

Holmes, P. R. (2006). Trinity in Human Community: Exploring Congregational Life in the Image of the Social Trinity. Bletchley, UK: Paternoster Press.

Jacob's Well Chicago. (n.d.). Who We Are. Retrieved April 11, 2016, from http://www.jacobswellchicago.com/#/different/

Johnson, S., (1998). Who Moved My Cheese? New York: G. P. Putman's Sons.

Jones, E. S. (1970). The Reconstruction of the Church—On What Pattern? Nashville, TN: Abingdon Press.

Kilde, J. H. (2002). When Church Became Theater: The Transformation of Evangelical Architecture and Worship in Nineteenth-Century America. New York, NY: Oxford University Press.

Kreider, A., & Kreider, E. (2011). Worship and Mission after Christendom. Harrisonburg, VA: Herald Press.

Ladd, G. E. (1959) The Gospel of the Kingdom. Grand Rapids, MI: Wm. B. Eerdmans Publishing Company.

Lausanne Committee for World Evangelization, "Marketplace Ministry, Occasional Paper No. 40." Retrieved July 9, 2010, https://www.lausanne.org/docs/2004forum/LOP40_IG11.pdf

Lindsley, A., Dr. (2013, October 15). The Priesthood of All Believers [Web log post]. Retrieved April 18, 2016, from https://tifwe.org/resource/the-priesthood-of-all-believers/

Marshall, I. H. (1985). How Far Did the Early Christians Worship God? Retrieved April 15, 2016, from http://churchsociety.org/docs/churchman/099/Cman_099_3_Marshall.pdf

Martinez, J. (2014, March 10). TD Jakes Tells Church Leaders 'If You're Not Making any Change, You're Taking Up Space [Web log post]. Retrieved April 16, 2016, from http://www.christianpost.com/news/td-jakes-tells-church-leaders-if-youre-not-making-any-change-youre-taking-up-space-115914/

McDonald's. Our Story. Retrieved January 23, 2016, from http://www.mcdonalds.com/us/en/our_story.html

McKay, B. (2011, August 28). Viewers vs. Doers: The Rise of Spectatoritis [Web log post]. Retrieved April 13, 2016, from http://www.artofmanliness.com/2011/08/28/viewers-vs-doers-the-rise-of-spectatoritis/

McKnight, T. (2014, November 6). 5 Reasons We Don't Make Disciples [Web log post]. Retrieved April 16, 2016, from http://auministry.com/5-reasons-disciples/

MennoMedia. (n.d.). The Heart of Mennonite Worship: Five Vital Rhythms [Online Study Guide]. Retrieved April 15, 2016, from http://www.mpn.net/worship/pdf/HoMW_1.pdf

Merriam-Webster Dictionary, Retrieved April 18, 2016, from http://www.merriam-webster.com/dictionary/centrifugal

Merriam-Webster Dictionary, Retrieved April 18, 2016, from http://www.merriam-webster.com/dictionary/centripetal

Mouw, R. J. (2011). Abraham Kuyper: A Short and Personal Introduction, Grand Rapids, MI: Wm. B. Eerdmans Publishing Co.

Murphy, E. F. (1972). The Gifts of the Spirit and the Mission of the Church. Pasadena, CA: Fuller Theological Seminary.

Murrow, D. (2015, June 2). Use the 10-10 format to teach men [Web log post]. Retrieved April 7, 2016, from http://www.patheos.com/blogs/churchformen/2015/06/use-the-10-10-format-to-teach-men/

Nash, J. B. (1932) Spectatoritis. New York: Holston House.

Network Church. (n.d.). Our Network Distinctives. Retrieved April 11, 2016, from http://www.networkchurch.org/Groups/248573/Network_Church/About_Us/Our_Distinctives/Our_Distinctives.aspx

New Day Church. (n.d.). Welcome. Retrieved April 13, 2016, from http://www.newdaynw.com/about/welcome/

Norrington, D. C. (1996). To Preach or Not to Preach? The Church's Urgent Question. Omaha, NE: Ekklesia Press.

Ogden, G. (1990). The New Reformation: Returning the Ministry to the People of God. Grand Rapids: Zondervan Publishing House.

Ogden, G. (2011, Spring). The Discipleship Deficit: Where Have all the Disciples Gone? Knowing & Doing, 2011, Spring. Retrieved April 16, 2016, from http://www.cslewisinstitute.org/The_Discipleship_Deficit_page1

Packard, J., & Hope, A. (2015). Church Refugees: Sociologists reveal why people are DONE with church but not their faith. Loveland, CO: Group Publishing.

Peterson, D., & Marshall, I. H. (1992). Engaging with God: a Biblical Theology of Worship. Downers Grove, IL: InterVarsity Press.

Peterson, E. (2011). The Jesus Way: A Conversation on the Ways That Jesus Is the Way. Grand Rapids, MI: William B. Eerdmans Publishing Co.

Platt, D. (Speaker) (n.d.). The Tragic Cost of Non-Discipleship [Video Podcast]. Retrieved April 16, 2016, from http://worship.com/2013/07/the-tragic-cost-of-non-discipleship-david-platt/

Preaching Today, "Dialogical Preaching (Part 1)" Retrieved April 13, 2016, from http://www.preachingtoday.com/skills/themes/energyofsynergy/dialogicalpreaching1.html

Pulpit Path to Stardom. Retrieved April 15, 2016, from https://news.google.com/newspapers?nid=1144&dat=19380703&id=ZisbAAAAIBAJ&sjid=BE0EAAAAIBAJ&pg=5835,5856598&hl=en

Rainier, T. S. (2014, November 3). Should Your Church Stop Having a Stand and Greet Time? [Web log post]. Retrieved June 6, 2016, from http://thomrainer.com/2014/11/church-stop-stand-greet-time/

Rainier, T.S. (2014, November 1), Top Ten Ways Churches Drive Away First-Time Guests [Web log post]. Retrieved April 16, 2016, from http://thomrainer.com/2014/11/top-ten-ways-churches-drive-away-first-time-guests/

Reju, D. The Politics of Terrorism [Web log post]. Retrieved July 11, 2016, from http://pastordot.blogspot.com/2010/01/politics-of-terrorism.html

Ritzer, G. F. (2007). The McDonaldization of Society. New York, NY: Sage Publications, Inc.

Ritzer, G. F. (2009). McDonaldization: The Reader. New York, NY: Sage Publications, Inc.

Rodriguez, M. (2004). The Priesthood of All Believers: 1st Century Church Life in the 21st Century. The Rebuilders.

Rothwell, R. (2009, October 20). Forgotten Providence - Ligonier Leadership Conference (I) [Web log post]. Retrieved April 18, 2016, from http://www.ligonier.org/blog/forgotten-providence-ligonier-leadership-conference-i/

Schultz, T. S. (2011, February 3). The Big New Spectator Sport: Church [Web log post]. Retrieved April 13, 2016, from http://holysoup.com/2011/02/03/the-big-new-spectator-sport-church/

Schultz, T. S. (2015, June 9). Done with 'Sit Down and Shut Up' [Web log post]. Retrieved April 16, 2016, from http://holysoup.com/2015/06/09/done-with-sit-down-and-shut-up/

Simms, S. (2011). Are Sermons Effective? [Web log post]. Retrieved April 12, 2016, from https://stevesimms.wordpress.com/2011/12/09/are-sermons-effective/

Smith, C. C. (2014, August 5). The Koinonia Way [Web Only Magazine Article]. Retrieved April 15, 2016, from http://www.christianitytoday.com/le/2014/august-online-only/koinonia-way.html

Stedman, R. (1972). Body Life. Glendale, CA: Regal Books Division, G/L Publications.

Stevens, R. P. (1999). The Other Six Days: Vocation, Work, and Ministry in Biblical Perspective. Grand Rapids, MI: Wm. B. Eerdmans Publishing Co.

Stevens, R. P. & Collins, P. (1993). The Equipping Pastor: A Systems Approach to Congregational Leadership. Durham, NC: The Alban Institute.

The Kingdom Citizens' Pavilion. (n.d.). Our Vision. Retrieved April 11, 2016, from http://www.thekingdomcitizensng.com/our-vision/

The Martin Luther King, Jr., Papers Project, "'Worship,' Sermon at Dexter Avenue Baptist Church." Retrieved June 6, 2016, from https://swap.stanford.edu/20141218225616/http://mlk-kpp01.stanford.edu/primarydocuments/Vol6/7Aug1955Worship.pdf

Thomson, J. (2003). Preaching as Dialogue: Is the Sermon a Sacred Cow? Cambridge, MA: Grove Books Limited.

Trueblood, D. (1967). The Incendiary Fellowship. New York: Harper & Row Publishers, Inc.

Tullos, M. (n.d.). 34 Tips for Creating Powerful Worship Experiences and Vibrant Worship Teams [Web log post]. Retrieved April 15, 2016, from https://louisianabaptists.org/34-tips-for-creating-powerful-worship-experiences-and-vibrant-worship-teams/

UK Parliament. Architecture of the Palace, "Churchill and the Commons Chamber." Retrieved April 15, 2016, from http://www.parliament.uk/about/living-heritage/building/palace/architecture/palacestructure/churchill/

Unger, Merrill F. (1961) Unger's Bible Dictionary, Chicago, IL: Moody Press.

U.S. Religion Census. (2010). U.S. Religion Census 2010: Summary Findings. Retrieved April 16, 2016, from http://www.rcms2010.org/press_release/ACP%2020120501.pdf

Vaters, K. (2015, February 16). 5 Cautions About Emphasizing Leadership over Followership. Retrieved April 15, 2016, from http://newsmallchurch.com/leadership-over-followership/

Wallenmeyer, M. (2012, December 11). Tag Archives: Reasons We Don't Make Disciples [Web log post]. Retrieved April 16, 2016, from http://michaelwallenmeyer.com/tag/reasons-we-dont-make-disciples/

Ward, K. (2015, March 6). If Form Follows Function, Perhaps We Need to Redesign Our Churches [Web log post]. Retrieved April 15, 2016, from http://www.churchinacircle.com/2015/03/06/if-form-follows-function-perhaps-we-need-to-redesign-our-churches/

Watson, D. (1979). I Believe in the Church. Grand Rapids, MI: Eerdmans Pub. Co.

Westview Bible Church, Retrieved April 13, 2016, from http://www.westviewlife.org/group-life

Willard, D. (1998). The Divine Conspiracy: Rediscovering Our Hidden Life in God. New York, NY: HarperCollins Publishers.

Willard, D. (2015). The Allure of Gentleness: Defending the Faith in the Manner of Jesus. New York, NY: HarperCollins Publishers.

Williams, S. M. (2008, March 3). Interactive Preaching [Web log post]. Retrieved January 30, 2016, from http://www.anabaptistnetwork.com/node/322

Williams, S., & Williams, S. M. (2012). The Power of All: Building a Multivoiced Church. Harrisburg, VA: Herald Press.

ABOUT THE AUTHOR

 Larry Peabody has served as a state employee, business owner, church planter, and senior pastor. He currently teaches theology of work courses for the Bakke Graduate University. He is the author of Serving Christ in the Workplace and Job-Shadowing Daniel: Walking the Talk at Work. He and his wife, Sharon, live in Lacey, Washington.

93685377R00137

Made in the USA
San Bernardino, CA
09 November 2018